GW00642986

Copyright © 2014 by Assembla, Inc.

All rights reserved. No part of this document may be reproduced in any form or by any electronic or mechanical means, including information storage and retrieval systems, without permission in writing from Assembla, Inc., except by a reviewer who may quote brief passages in a review.

Assembla is a trademark of Assembla, Inc. All other trademarks are the property of their respective owners.

Table Of Contents

Introduction

Why Continuous Agile?

The long-awaited software revolution is upon us. Small startups deliver "minimum viable products" in a few weeks and then evolve them. Huge phone companies win billions if they can beat the competition to market with software ecosystems and infrastructure. Top online services employ thousands of developers, each empowered to release changes multiple times per week. Large-scale intelligent systems respond to your questions, drive your car, and then learn what to do tomorrow.

This revolution is being powered by new trends in software development:

- **Global teams** - Not just outsourced teams that sit together in remote locations, but teams that are truly dispersed across the globe. The sun never sets on this empire of code.

- **Code contribution techniques** - Methods to collect code improvements from one contributor, or from thousands, refined over the last 20 years in a vast range of open source projects.

- **Cloud computing** - On-demand build and test systems that are the underlying engine of release speed.

- **Rapid competitive evolution** - Online products that respond quickly to competitors and partners, driven by daily releases and rapid adjustments instead of long-range product planning.

My SaaS company, Assembla, helps customers manage cloud-based teams and take advantage of these trends. However, our own software development techniques were not keeping up. In the fall of 2011 we had problems:

- Releases took longer as our system got bigger and there was more to test. Our two week cycle release became three weeks or more as we spent more time on testing and bug fixing.

- Releases were stressful. After a release, we found bugs in production. Actually, our users found the bugs, and then demanded that we fix them immediately.

- Competitors were achieving faster velocity with Continuous Delivery, which is a way of saying that they were kicking our butts.

The answer to our problems would not come from normal companies figuring out "best of breed" versions of the old Agile practices. We saw how Agile techniques like Scrum had helped small teams gain confidence by answering questions like "what tasks will we work on together?" But we also saw that Scrum didn't work in a distributed, cloud-based environment. It did not take full advantage of modern automation, it was confined to release iterations of a week or longer, and handicapped by reliance on Post-it notes and face-to-face, meat-to-meat interactions. Scrum failed to accommodate global teams, big projects, and rapid releases.

Instead, we studied industry leaders who are knocking the stuffing out of their competitors (some of their stories are included in this book). They do Continuous Delivery, and they have solved these problems. But we didn't start our company with Continuous Delivery. We had to study it, learn it, and build it up incrementally with tools and skills.

We began implementing this approach in early 2012, using the philosophy of "release more frequently" and incremental improvement. The results are posted below. Now we release changes about 250 times per month. We have fewer bugs in production. Without big releases, we have much less stress.

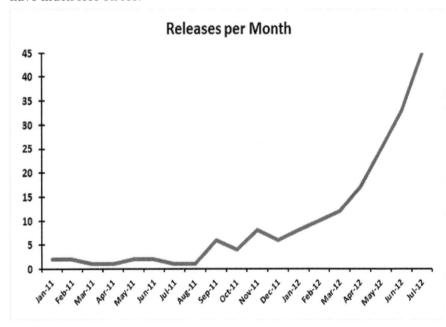

We found a new type of "Continuous Agile" software development that is:

- **Continuous and non-blocking**: Team members can work on their own features without waiting for someone else to debug and release, permitting each person to work in an efficient way, while at the same time allowing projects to scale to hundreds (or for some open source projects, thousands) of contributors.

- **Lean**: Contributors can work on one task at a time, do a good job, and finish it. Managers can "pull what's ready" to assemble a release.

- **Automated**: Nothing is hidden in manual build commands or Post-it note plans; everything gets put into repeatable scripts and is visible online.

- **Based on managing code**: It is important to manage people, but it is easier to manage code. The new Continuous Agile makes extensive use of source code management and code contribution workflows. It adds code management to the old team and task management.

You will need these techniques if you provide any type of online service, or if you have a big project with a lot of contributors, or if you are running a lean startup.

This type of development is powering the most successful online services. When we looked more closely, we found that continuous delivery was also powering larger IT operations. They are using a revolutionary technique to release tens of thousands of adjustments in the time that a competitor does one release. Almost all business products and services are now built on software and IT systems. To compete, you will need to release more frequently.

What you will get from this book

This book will help you win with more frequent releases. It will share what we learned at Assembla, and what market-winning companies have told us about their success in moving toward Continuous Delivery and Continuous Agile. It contains terms that will help you discuss your strategy and tactics with your development teams, managers, partners, and investors. You will learn about "test layering," "feature switches," "unveil," "learn before launch," and many other tactics.

In this guide you will find:

An overview of Agile techniques for task management, code management, and testing. Most people find one method that works and stick to it like dogma. We will show you more options. The overview will make you a smarter software developer who can **pick the right tactics**, and switch tactics at the right time.

Continuous Delivery. When I first heard about Kanban with continuous delivery - releasing every change - I thought it was magic. How would you test it? The answers are very practical. We break continuous delivery into components you can adopt.

A way to evolve your project from simple roadmapping and prototyping all the way to full continuous release. This is the "**beyond scrum roadmap**." It provides a high-speed alternative to more laborious project planning.

Recommendations for handling the new world of **distributed teams** and team building.

Revolutionary techniques to solve the most expensive problem in tech: **scaling to larger teams** and working productively in big software projects.

Continuous product management that will help your business keep up with your accelerating continuous development.

You will also find unique opinions that I have developed over decades of working with startup teams, pushing the boundaries of Internet technology starting in 1994, moving to SaaS in 1998, and building out distributed teams on the 2000's. This isn't the same corporate agile BS. It comes from first principles.

To round off these insights, we have included stories from other organizations that figured out how to thrash their competitors by releasing more frequently. Co-authors contributed ideas and chapters that expanded my understanding.

It is with great satisfaction that I present this guide to Continuous Agile. It connects innovations in Continuous Delivery with the traditions of Agile, in a way that is compatible with existing Scrum teams, but also works for modern, cloud-based teams.

Continuous Agile

About Agile

At one time software projects were planned like construction projects, marching forward one phase at a time in sequence, ending with a complete delivery of the finished building or piece of software. We called this a "waterfall" process because the effort cascaded out of one phase into the next.

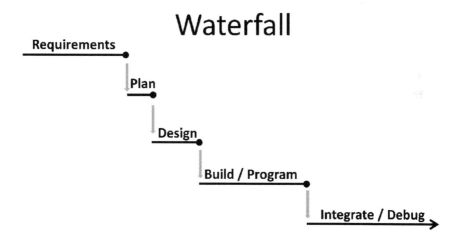

Waterfall projects suffered from two big sources of delay. The first source of delay was in the requirements phase. It was hard to figure out everything that application users wanted to do in the future. Projects tended to have a long "fuzzy front end" period to work out requirements. A project might never get started if requirements kept changing.

The second source of delay was in the integration and debugging phase. The components of a large project rarely worked together as expected, and the integration phase could be longer than expected (and sometimes infinite).

With a waterfall project, you ran the risk that the project would never start, or never finish. That is why the world moved to Agile.

Agile projects get started faster and get to integration faster. The Agile lifecycle starts with a short phase of roadmapping and prototyping. After that the system proceeds directly to a series of short build and release cycles.

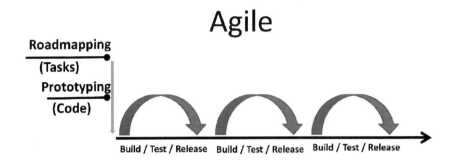

Repetition leads to efficiency. Agile projects have higher productivity because a much bigger part of their lifetime is spent in programming iterations. Developers have time to optimize and automate so that each iteration is more productive than the last.

While a waterfall project is intended to be finished and delivered, an Agile project is never really done. Agile projects have an evolutionary lifecycle rather than a plan. The variable scope can be used to make products that are better than the original requirements.

All Agile methodologies depend on frequent releases. This eliminates the risk of non-delivery, and lowers the risk of bad results. Each release resolves integration problems. It also provides an opportunity for end users to see the product and provide feedback, so the development team can receive detailed, up-to-date information on real user requirements.

In order to guarantee frequent releases, most Agile methodologies release on a fixed schedule, rather than when features are finished.

We can imagine the development of a software feature as a sequence of steps, from figuring out what to do (the fuzzy front end), to defining the required tasks and assigning them to team members (task management), to changing code (code contribution), to building, testing and deploying the result.

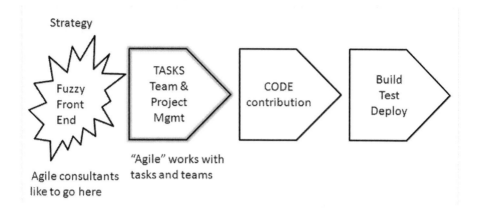

The many variants of Agile are different types of team and task management, so traditional "Agile" methodologies only take advantage of one piece of the puzzle.

The most popular methodology is Scrum, which engages "self-managing" teams of 5 to 10 people. They plan and deliver software in iterations that are typically 2-6 weeks long. The process can be very motivating for team members, and it provides a framework for regular process improvement. For these reasons, Scrum is extremely popular in large organizations, crowding out other Agile methodologies.

Scrum will probably work well for you if your teams meet these requirements:

- Your teams are all 5 to 10 people.

- Each team is co-located and meets in person every day.

- They implement with iterations that are two to four weeks long.

- You release software every four to 26 weeks.

However, I rarely see these conditions in cloud-based development. Teams sticking to Scrum will have problems:

- Releasing rapidly.

- Scaling to distributed groups.

- Engaging large numbers of new contributors.

Fortunately, there is a continuous form of Agile development that works better for frequent releases, distributed teams, and large and diverse groups of contributors. Continuous Agile pulls in new ideas from coding workflows, code review, automated testing, and continuous integration. These produce much faster release cycles and more scalable teams. And when we get to build, test, and deploy methods, we find an avalanche of new capabilities from cloud computing providers.

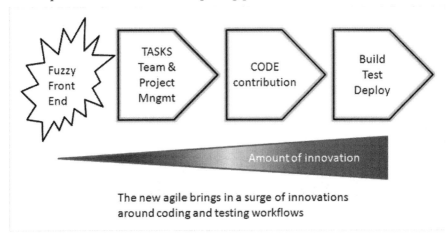

The new agile brings in a surge of innovations around coding and testing workflows

Continuous Agile Principles

We use "Continuous Agile" to describe the combination of **Kanban Agile task management** with **continuous delivery code management**.

"Agile" traditionally describes task and team management. We get two big advantages from bringing code management into the process. First, we can actually finish a Kanban task by merging, testing, and deploying code. Second, we can bring in a lot of innovations from the rapidly advancing art of code contribution and testing.

Building blocks

There are many successful routes. We will try to break away from the bad habits of people who find one thing that worked for them, and then recommend it for everyone else. This guide describes a set of building blocks to choose from.

Task management: The spectrum of task management tactics begins with roadmapping (making a list) and continues to planning releases with batches of tasks, and then to continuous or Kanban. Users often adopt these in sequence.

Code management: Code management with a repository is the core technology of continuous delivery. We find that practitioners can succeed with a "centralized" process that makes all contributions and tests on one version, or a "distributed' process where contributions are tested on separate versions. This is supported by the rapidly advancing art of contributing, reviewing, and merging code.

Testing: You want to very quickly test a change to prepare it for release, and you want to do this in the most efficient way possible, and you want your culture to support the testing. Testing and test automation is the most important investment that you will make in the move to continuous agile.

Product Management: You will accelerate planning to keep up with your developers, unblock them so they can work and release without waiting, and follow each individual change as it flows to release.

Team leaders should understand all of the options, not just the familiar ones. They should change tactics when they run into obstacles, delays, and new opportunities.

Lean principles

We want to build software faster and with less stress. Continuous Agile uses some "lean" principles to achieve this goal:

- Continuous improvement. Have a periodic engineering review and happiness survey. Measure results and improve measurements.

- Make batches of work smaller until you drive the unit of change down toward "one-piece flow"; release every change when it is ready. Do not stop at two-week batches.

- Use the principle of pull, where each worker or team pulls a task when they are ready to work on it.

- Limit the number of active tasks - called "Work in Progress." This improves focus, predictability, and speed.

- Use a "pull what is ready" approach to assembling releases. Releases do not need to be planned in advance and assembled under stress. You can prioritize at the beginning, and "plan" (assemble) releases at the end.

- Manage code and not people if possible. Code is easier to manage at scale. People (contributors) are hard to manage, but they will contribute code if you give them a path.

- Automate to increase human productivity by using more machines.

- Increase productivity by skipping steps and rituals. It is surprising how often you can get the same result with less work.

There is no single correct process or set of tactics. We present a toolbox of task and code management options. Teams select a process and tactics to fit their unique situation.

Three Agile Use Cases

When we surveyed Agile teams, we found three Agile use cases that were each quite different.

1) Online services. These are providers of Web, SaaS, big data, and mobile services. They live in a competitive, rapidly evolving environment. They talk a lot about release frequency, testing, and automation, and much less about building permanent teams. They need to release quickly to avoid being crushed by competitors that release more frequently. We believe that **most online service providers will move to continuous delivery and continuous Agile**.

2) Long-cycle releases, every three, six, or twelve months. Leaders of these projects were happy with iterative or Scrum tactics. They talked a lot about building teams, which is an important focus of Scrum. If they move to continuous Agile, it is because their product is taking too long to test and release, or they want to increase the scale of development.

3) Service providers. These are consultants, outsourcers, design agencies, and corporate IT shops who have many clients to satisfy. Typically they have more projects than teams. Their concern was with prioritizing incoming requests, and with allocating resources. They frequently ask "who is available?" and they find it impractical to run a permanent Scrum team for each project. However, they can run short Agile release cycles with minimal rituals. We will show how to negotiate and deliver a continuous agile service project.

Embedded systems development is a fourth use case that we didn't cover in our survey. Many embedded systems developers use a "cadence" system where they put the parts together at fixed X-week intervals. Hardware changes are released infrequently, so this is almost the same as the long-cycle release case. However, I believe that the best embedded developers can unblock and accelerate by delivering new software builds daily. They can use "unveil" techniques to hide new software and hardware, until they are ready to be switched on in tandem.

The Beyond Scrum Roadmap

Some IT shops often make the mistake of trying to fit all projects into one development process. In fact, this is the primary focus of many Agile and quality initiatives. However, it doesn't work, because the projects are actually different. A new experimental project is not the same as a big mature project. An application for a marketing campaign needs to move fast. Billing system development should be slower, secure and reliable.

Fortunately, many projects go through some predictable stages of life. If you think of software as having a lifecycle and not a plan, you will have projects that are more efficient at each stage of life. This is the idea behind the Beyond Scrum Roadmap. It illustrates some typical patterns of task management and code management.

Roadmapping and prototyping

Almost all projects start with roadmapping. You write down everything that you want to deliver. This is sometimes called brainstorming. You then sort those things in priority order. Finally, you take the top deliverables and form them into a minimum useful release. This gives you a vision of the completed system, a rough plan (roadmap) showing the order of delivery, and most importantly, your marching orders for the first release.

All projects should start with prototyping. You quickly and informally build a system to test technical possibilities and your assumptions about what will be useful.

My rule of prototyping is to use one person, or a very small team. Prototyping should be a cheap way to try anything new. It is an essential tool for any kind of innovation, in any stage company.

At this point, you are in continuous delivery paradise: just code it and show it. But your product will not be reliable.

Scrum with release branches and release candidates

After people start using your software, you want to test it before you release it. You will move to iterative releases, where you take the time to build a release candidate and test it. You might even decide to move all the way to Scrum because of the good feedback that it provides for small teams. This is not paradise. It is annoying to take big chunks of time to fix bugs and deliver complete features. However, your users will like the result.

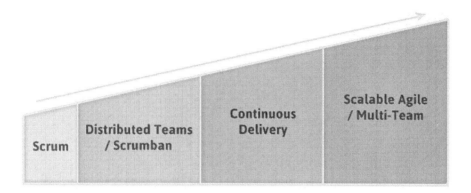

Scrumban and Continuous Integration

If you have distributed teams or barriers to in-person planning, you will want to move to Scrumban, a planning approach that combines Scrum with lean concepts. It is a simple change: just skip the iteration plan and pull tasks when you are ready to work on them. You will start moving back toward continuous paradise.

However, you need to do some real work to get to paradise. You may find that it takes longer and longer to test and release each iteration, because your software contains more things to test. When this happens, you can solve the problem with continuous, automated testing. You will need to deploy the technical underpinnings of a continuous integration system, and move to a social structure that encourages your developers to build and run tests every day.

If you are doing long-cycle releases, you will probably stay with this pattern. You can add more teams with a "cadence" tactic, where every team releases on the same schedule.

Kanban and Continuous Delivery

If you need speed and responsiveness, you will want to take the next step to fully continuous delivery. You will be able to assemble releases whenever you want with a "take what is ready" approach. This helps you to build software faster and reduce stress at the same time. Small fixes will go through in hours or days, and big changes will take an appropriate amount of time.

You will use a Kanban technique to manage your development tasks. In the Kanban approach, you pull one task at a time to work on, and you use lean techniques to make sure that it gets finished as quickly as possible. You will need to be sure that you do all of the normal planning, architecture and design for that task, but you will do it as needed, unblocked by other parts of your schedule. You may need to change how you do product management.

You will use continuous delivery processes to test and deploy each code change. These may require innovations in automation and testing. You may find that you are giving developers more authority, adding new test pipelines, and changing the role of your QA team.

Scaling with services

With all of that unblocked planning and automated testing, you are ready to increase the size and diversity of your development team and your applications. You can accept contributions from partners, outsourcers and new enthusiasts. You can test the contributions, take what is ready, and assemble the releases that you want.

We will describe the "matrix of services" or "MAXOS" structure that the best tech companies use to scale the speed, size, and complexity of their software development and IT operations.

Here is a slide that shows the stages of the roadmap from the point of view of a team that starts with Scrum.

Beyond Scrum

Scrum	Scrumban / Distributed	Continuous Delivery	Scalable Agile
Iterative releases with batch planning	Iterative releases without batch planning.	Release when ready	Add people or add complete teams
5 to 10 people in one place	Distributed teams	Pull and finish one task	Evaluate and report on contributors
	Add automated tests. Code review enforces test coverage	On-demand test and stage environments with full continuous integration.	Assemble releases on-demand from code contributions and separate services

We will discuss these concepts in more depth in the next sections of this guide.

Continuous Delivery

Benefits and Costs

Continuous delivery is a way to build software faster, with less stress. It brings together all of the capabilities that we discuss below: task management, code management, and automated testing.

When to use continuous delivery

You should use continuous delivery if:

You provide an online service: Web, SaaS, PaaS, online gaming, online big data, or mobile apps with Web service back ends. If you provide online services, you need to move to continuous delivery, or your competitors will race ahead of you.

Your release times are getting longer and longer. As your app gets more complicated, you may find that it takes longer to test and release. This is a sign that you should move to automated testing, continuous integration, and continuous delivery.

You are developing a new product and using lean startup techniques to test and evolve it.

You have a big project with a lot of contributors. Batch management will often fail in this case. Continuous delivery techniques will help you accept contributions from a large and diverse group of contributors, inside and outside of your core organization.

You need to release frequent security patches. Bad guys out there want to manipulate our systems to show ads, run compute-intensive algorithms, steal passwords and financial information, and view commercial and government secrets. With Chinese hackers going against the NSA, it's literally spy versus spy. We are caught in the crossfire, forced to issue frequent updates. You can think of continuous delivery as extending your security patch process to your software development activities.

Benefits

Speed: You get faster delivery of the most important improvements and fixes. You can release some changes in hours or days. When you fix problems faster, your system will have fewer bugs. You can accelerate delivery of a few great improvements, learn fast, and beat the competition.

Quality: I am often asked: "Does continuous delivery require me to release more quickly, with lower quality? Will I be releasing more bugs, and features with less refined usability?" Actually, continuous delivery gives you extra capacity that you can use to improve either speed or quality. You can choose to release faster, or you can choose to hold features longer before releasing and "unveiling" them, to move them to higher quality and usability. At Assembla, we found that our feature delivery got slower when we improved the usability of our software. Continuous delivery also results in systems with fewer bugs at any given time, because bugs are discovered and fixed faster.

Capacity and Scale: You can include a bigger, more scalable development team in a continuous process. Batch processes like iteration planning, release planning, and release testing become exponentially harder to organize as you involve an increasing number of people. With continuous delivery, we solve this problem by skipping batch processes. With the code contribution workflows listed here, you can manage code and not people, and accept the code that is ready. Code is easier to manage. You can organize thousands of people and hundreds of systems with continuous delivery. Also, you can work with an entire world of talent, because you can manage distributed teams effectively.

Cost: You spend less money and time on meetings and management. If you eliminate batch processes you don't need as many big, expensive meetings.

Focus: Team members have more time to think. Developers can completely finish and release a task before they move to the next task. They do not need to switch their brains and their configurations between tasks. Product managers and QA people also get this benefit.

Clarity: Your team should experience less stress. With continuous delivery, you fix small problems quickly. Bigger changes take only as long as the work requires, because they are not delayed by stops and starts. You have fewer high-pressure spikes of release work. You can think about one thing at a time. All of these factors lower stress so that you can have a better life and work more effectively.

Costs

Continuous delivery requires you to set up and administer automated testing. You will need to write automated tests, and you will need to automate the configuration of test environments. In our experience, automating testing takes more time and effort than any other aspect of a continuous delivery rollout.

In an experimental product, you can push some of the costs of testing onto users. We'll talk about this option when we cover testing and product management.

Continuous delivery also involves developer training costs. Developers need to understand the details of their version control system. They need a full social commitment to automated testing. They must take more responsibility for delivering release-ready code and features.

Incremental releases are complicated. Developers must figure out how to insert major changes invisibly, and hide them with switches until they are ready to be released. This staged migration adds some complexity that is not present if you just rip out the old stuff and then test the new stuff. However, you will gain confidence by seeing changes working in production systems before you "unveil" them to your users. This can more than compensate for the increased complexity.

Foundations

As you move toward continuous delivery, you will incrementally improve each of these foundation capabilities:

Developer responsibility: Developers will approve releases. It is the responsibility of the developers to make sure that their code doesn't break anything. Their code should be releasable. They can't just throw it over to QA and wait for bug reports. They will be motivated to write automated tests. Developers will make decisions about what to release. QA professionals should serve in a consulting role to help developers as needed.

Feature switches: Developers can release code for new features continuously by hiding features that aren't ready. When you are adding significant new features or making architecture changes, you will in most cases be running both old and new versions of your software at the same time. In following chapters we will cover the hiding and "unveil" tactics that make it possible to smoothly sneak big changes into a continuously released system.

Code contribution: You will want to use one of the continuous delivery code contribution patterns described here - centralized, distributed, or hybrid.

Test Layering: You will learn how to add layers of tests so that you can be confident that every change will work well on release. You will want enough automated tests to tell you immediately if something is broken. You run them frequently. You log and monitor your running software to see errors and understand usage. You will add tests and test layers when you need to increase quality, or you will remove tests and test layers to increase speed.

Automated builds: Manually building and distributing software takes too much time and results in too many errors. You will need scripts to build and deploy your software. And, if you want to release more frequently, you need someone to release to.

Continuous Improvement: You do not need all of these things to release more frequently. You can move to continuous delivery incrementally, in two simple steps.

1. Release more frequently

2. Improve

Changing Roles

Moving from batch releases to fast, continuous delivery processes drives changes in roles. When developers release more frequently, development starts overrunning the other roles, and you have to adjust.

	Plan	Design	Code	Test and Approve	Deploy	Unveil	Measure	Tools
Before	Product Manager or Owner	UX Designer	Developer	QA	Ops	Product Manager	?	Ops Dev
After	Senior Manager	Story Owner UX Developer Requests	Developer	Developer QA Consults Story Owner on usability	Dev	Story Owner	Story Owner Dev	DevOps
Control			Developer →					
		Story Owner →						

Developers and programmers

Developers gain a lot of power and a lot of responsibility from continuous delivery.

Developers (programmers) will decide what is ready to release. **This is a strong finding**. We see it in all successful continuous delivery organizations. The developer of a feature decides when it is ready, and runs the scripts to put it into the production version.

This happens for two reasons:

1. It is faster. You unblock your team so that developers can work at full speed. They don't have to wait for a product manager, product owner, or marketing person to tell them that users, marketing and documentation are ready for a release. Instead, they release everything that is ready, and hide it from the general public. The PM or marketing person can come along later, see that the new feature works, and start the "unveil" process.

2. It provides the correct incentives. The developer is responsible for the release, because he or she is the one who can fix it. A developer can be called back from Friday night beers to fix a problem. Therefore, developers have a compelling reason to make a good decision about what to release. They should not throw buggy code over the all to a QA person. They need to be

forced to focus on quality by removing the QA training wheels. They will be motivated to build good tests, and good scripts for testing and deployment.

Developers will have more responsibility for testing. They will write and run automated tests. They will get whatever help they need to make sure a change is released without bugs.

DevOps

DevOps is the hot new role required in a continuous delivery process. A DevOps professional is a system operator and administrator who also knows how to write scripts to automate testing, deployment, and measurement. You will need this. You can get it from operations, from developers, or both.

Ideally, DevOps should not be responsible for builds and releases. Developers should make builds and releases, using tools that they develop with the ops team. The DevOps movement is about providing automated tools. Essentially, they package the things that your operations guys used to do manually into convenient SaaS services.

In a big shop there will be DevOps people who specialize in building test systems, running tests, and reporting on test results, code quality, and developer contributions. This is the Test Engineering team.

QA and testers

QA acts as a consultant to the developers. Developers will call in a QA professional to make sure that a change does not cause problems, and is a good change. They need the QA professional to protect against mistakes, clarify requirements, and cover their butts.

QA gets more respect! Developers appreciate QA expertise more when they have to ask for it.

In a distributed continuous delivery process, the QA team members might find that there are multiple test systems, and they need to look in multiple places for the version that they are going to test.

A good QA team will learn to build and run automated tests. QA team members will spend more time doing usability testing and exploratory testing. The developers are busy making sure they don't release bugs. This frees up QA to figure out if the debugged features are actually useful. Also, more features will be released in some sort of improvement process before they are unveiled.

QA should also be freed up to monitor and measure the quality and productivity of the development process. So, they give up power over specific releases, but they get influence over the whole development process.

With developers and DevOps taking more responsibility, it is normal to have a fairly high ratio of engineers to testers - more than 5 to 1. This reverses the pathology that a lot of companies get into. They find that releases are taking longer and longer to test, so they add more and more test professionals, until finally they have as many testers as programmers. This tactic can marginally increase quality. However, it cannot accelerate delivery, because the testers only find problems. The problems still need to be fixed. By moving to continuous delivery with more layers of review and testing BEFORE software goes to QA, companies fix the problem at its source and eliminate release delays while freeing up QA capacity.

Product managers and product owners

Product managers and product owners are supposed to decide what features will go in the product, and what those features will look like. A full-speed continuous delivery development team will run past them and run over them. If the development team gets going too fast they will start to implement stories that product owners have never refined, or even approved, and they will produce features with no value. Product owners need a way to make sure that every feature implemented is a great feature.

Our solution is to ask product owners to work more closely with the developers during design and implementation of a story. When they take this role, we call them "story owners." This matches the speed of development with the speed of design. It helps get stories into development faster, because they require less up-front design. Story owners, designers and developers can start working on incremental design and implementation of a story when they have a clear use case to guide their design and implementation. This tactic also slows down development to enforce quality. Developers, designers and product owners can take as much time as they require before unveiling new features.

We see some other big changes in the role of product managers and product owners.

Usability is more important than requirements. A product that nobody uses doesn't meet anyone's requirements. Modern product owners should become experts in usability. Usability can be shaped from day to day based on feedback from frequent releases.

Measurements are supplementing or replacing strategy and market research. Product owners should be driven by metrics. Modern systems produce a lot of performance and usage numbers. These numbers can be a more effective guide than other types of feedback and market research.

Senior managers

Experiment. Limit the size of new projects. Make them earn bigger budgets and bigger rollouts. Don't expect new projects to meet the same quality and process requirements as mature projects. Let new projects be small and experimental with phases for prototyping, and beta testing. I call this "learn before launch."

Fund. Senior managers should not budget for specific features or releases. That slows everything down to negotiating and fulfilling a fixed plan. Unblock! by funding the team or product or program. Later, you can allocate capacity. Out of the stories that are on the Kanban board, a certain percentage can come from each epic, product owner or initiative that the company is supporting.

Measure. Managers should measure velocity, and look for bottlenecks in overall delivery of value. They should ask for frequent measurements of the development process, and of product usage.

Prioritize and Limit WIP. Make big plans and keep a big backlog, but work on a small number of things at the same time. If your team is working on a lot of different things, they will not be able to take any new requests. They will be unresponsive. IT organizations often become unresponsive because they have too many active projects. Working on a small number of tasks, and having some free capacity, will increase the speed and responsiveness of any organization, large or small. Senior managers will get responsiveness if they do their jobs and prioritize.

Indulge. Managers can indulge in making a few high priority requests. The continuous delivery capability can give them rapid delivery of features and fixes. It is a powerful tool. But it will only work for a small number of requests at one time. And, it will only work if the team has room for the rush requests, because they have a limited number of other requests.

Accelerate. They should be looking for opportunities to use continuous techniques in other areas of the company. Once development gets rolling, they can accelerate launch, marketing, budgeting and hiring.

Feature Switches

You can work on features and architecture changes that take months to finish, yet still release your code every day. You accomplish this with "feature switches" that hide new features.

Feature switches can go directly into your code as IF statements that detect the type of user or system running the code. Typically, they have four states:

Hidden: Nobody sees the feature.

Test: Only internal testers on internal test systems see the feature.

Beta: Beta test users and systems see the feature.

Full release or "Unveil": Everyone sees the feature.

The "Unveil" is the big event, the final release. Hooray! It is the definition of done.

The unveil technique is what allows us to unblock. Developers can build and release hidden features without waiting for product owners (or story owners, or product managers, or the CEO) to approve a release. Your design team can do usability testing with beta users. The unveil can be scheduled when the product owner, marketing team, and everyone else is ready, long after the developers have moved on to other tasks.

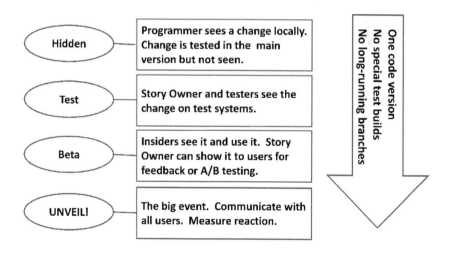

Everyone does it

Web application developers often use feature switches to turn on features for specific types of users or user accounts.

Assembla employees usually find themselves running beta features not yet unveiled to customers.

A bank developer told me that when he puts his card into an ATM, he gets a menu with new beta test choices not shown to regular account holders.

Hardware vendors often leave empty sockets in their computers, phones and other devices that can be filled later with new components. Semiconductor companies leave space on chips, or even complete circuits that are switched off.

Software installed locally on clients and servers sometimes has hidden features that can be unlocked by special keys, either when a new feature is fully tested or when the customer pays an upgrade fee. Developers of client and mobile apps can expose new services to particular user types.

Wherever you find rapid development, you will find feature switches.

No long-running feature branches

Today, contributors sometimes keep many changes in an isolated version of the code and then merge and release all of them at once. They do this to avoid the interruptions that would come from users seeing and reacting to each change individually.

This results in the dreaded Long-Running Feature Branch. The Long-Running Feature Branch allows the contributor to work undisturbed and make many changes without interruption. However, it creates serious problems. While your contributor is working, you can't easily see his work and manage or help him. When he merges the changes back into the main version, it creates a lot of bugs. Often the merge itself requires a lot of manual labor to interweave changes that were made during the Long Run. It's hard to find and fix bugs because you have so much new code to look through.

If you use feature switches, you can eliminate Long-Running Feature Branches.

Advantages of switches

After you add switches you can take frequent small changes from every contributor. There will be fewer bugs in each contribution, and the bugs are much easier to find because you have less new code to look through.

Contributor work is visible and measurable. You never wonder why someone disappeared for a month.

Deployment and the test infrastructure can be simplified. You don't need a special deployment of a branch version for "beta.myproduct.com" or a special download. Features can be turned on for specific test, beta, or release installations, or for specific users.

Unblock! Developers can release features without being blocked by testers or product management. They can work and release at full speed by hiding new features, letting the other groups unveil features after test, marketing and other issues are addressed.

Features can be deployed incrementally. You can deploy significant changes to data structure and infrastructure bit by bit, testing changes and receiving feedback at a controlled pace.

The final "unveil" release is much less stressful and more reliable, because new features have been integrated, tested, and deployed (for some audiences) for some time before the unveil.

Life of a switch

Setup: You will need a few <condition> functions which tell you about deployment configurations and user accounts, so you can control who sees your feature.

Install: Put your switches into the menu or top service level, so you don't have to scatter them deeper in the code. You should be able to run unit tests without hitting the switches. Use a switch at the same level with a matching IF NOT <condition> to switch off the old feature when the time comes.

Overlap: You can deploy both versions, and possibly run automated tests for both versions. You can incrementally deploy changes to data structure and infrastructure as well as features. With experience, you can run both versions of your feature, data structure, or architecture. This seems complicated, but in most cases it is simpler and less stressful than releasing many new features to everyone in a big bang.

In fact, by allowing new and old features to overlap in one set of code you can answer the classic question "how do you change the engines while the plane is flying?"

Unveil: When everyone is happy, you turn on the feature for all audiences and unveil.

Remove: After new features have been unveiled to everyone, reduce the number of lines of maintained code by deleting the switches and obsolete code.

When you use feature switches there is a little bit of extra work to add the switches, test two versions of the code during the overlap period, and remove the switches. However, on balance you save work because your developers are unblocked and because the release is fully tested and deployed before you unveil.

Test Layering

"How do I test it?" is the fundamental question in any continuous release or Kanban process. We make batch releases so that we can test everything in the release. If we take away the release testing phase, we need some special magic to make sure we aren't releasing bugs.

Actually, we don't use magic. We use test layering. Any change passes through a series of tests. Together, these tests filter out most of the problems.

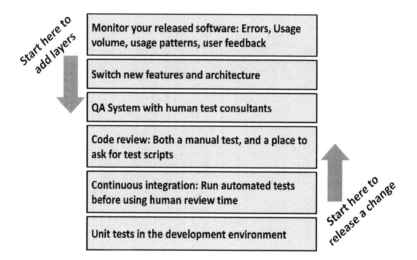

Test Layering

Start here to add layers

Monitor your released software: Errors, Usage volume, usage patterns, user feedback
Switch new features and architecture
QA System with human test consultants
Code review: Both a manual test, and a place to ask for test scripts
Continuous integration: Run automated tests before using human review time
Unit tests in the development environment

Start here to release a change

You can use this layering idea to increase quality, or increase speed. The continuous process doesn't inherently release more bugs than a batch testing process. It gives you a choice.

- You can add more layers or more tests to increase quality. You would do this if you see a quality problem, or if your product has more and more users who rely on it. For example, we found that when we moved to continuous delivery, we held features longer in the "switch new features" layer, so that we could improve design and usability.

- You can remove layers to increase speed. Use this technique to accelerate an early stage project.

You will want to add testing where it is most efficient. When adding tests, many people will start at the top of the stack above, by monitoring a production release, or at least collecting bug reports. That's a type of test. They may add manual or automated regression testing to that so that they find problems before customers find them. Then they will add unit tests, so that anyone working on code can check it. In practice, you will add layers going backward from the production release in order to find errors closer and closer to the time when the code changed.

Any individual change runs through these layers from the bottom to the top.

Let's look at some typical test layers, in the order that a developer will use them to test a change.

1. If your developers are writing unit test scripts, they will run the test scripts locally to make sure that they have not broken anything obvious. When working on a big system, programmers will select a subset of tests to run.

2. After the programmer submits code to the VCS, a continuous integration system can pick it up and run a bigger set of automated test scripts. It's useful to run these tests before code review, so that people don't waste time reviewing changes that failed tests.

3. Code review makes the whole process work. The reviewer will do a manual test, and will also look for standards compliance and automated test coverage. The reviewer can ask for automated tests if they are missing. If you want your programmers to write automated tests, you will probably need to require code review. If you require code review, you have a good chance of getting code that meets standards for style, architecture, and test coverage.

4. Changes will go to a system where human testers can look at them and run more extensive tests. Story owners, tech leads, and QA professionals will look at the change. QA professionals are typically called on when developers need them in a consulting role.

5. New features will be released, but hidden with feature switches. New features may go through an extended period where they are switched on selectively for beta testing, usability testing, or A/B testing.

6. The released software is monitored for errors, changes in usage, bug reports, and other user feedback.

Reversible and Risk Free

You want your changes to be reversible, and risk free. Nothing is risk free, but your changes will be low risk if you can reverse them. Then, you can make more changes, and have more fun.

Code

This is a solved problem. SCM systems make your code changes reversible. Use a good SCM system and understand your code contribution process.

Servers

Making server changes reversible is more challenging.

- Roll back. At the very minimum, you should always be able to roll back any production change or distribution, with a script.

- Later, you should be able to build the current version of any server, on demand.

- Finally, you might want to be able to build any version of any server, with a test database, etc.

Data

Don't change your schema by prematurely changing or overwriting data. Instead, add new fields, and make new copies of data. You can always reverse by ignoring it. Storage is cheap compared with peace of mind.

Features

You should be able to switch new features on and off. If a feature causes a problem or a negative response, you can turn it off. This capability is also useful through the entire development and testing process.

Thoughts and mental commitment

Tactical: If a change causes a problem, do not try to fix it on the fly. Reverse it, and fix it in a thoughtful way. This is a big change for some people.

Strategic: Do not cling to your ideas. Nothing is constant except change.

CD Dial

You can benefit from continuous delivery even if you can't release frequently. Maybe your customers will only accept a release once per quarter, or once per year. You may have strict regulatory or security requirements for testing. Maybe Apple will only let you release an app once every two weeks.

Developers can still reduce stress and increase focus by running a continuous delivery process inside the programming team. They can run a continuous agile process with Kanban, continuous integration, and test layering, and anything else that makes them fast and agile. They just need to make sure that the build is stable and high quality when the release team needs it.

Periodically, the release team will grab a release candidate from the development mainline and run that release candidate through a test and release process. You can select the point where you drop versions from continuous delivery into a batch release process. You can think of this as moving a dial - the CD Dial.

My friends Steve Brodie and Rohit Jainendra made this picture of a CD Dial when they were at Serena. In the diagram below, the CD Dial is set to run continuous delivery through development, test and integration. At that point the Ops people grab a release candidate and run it through staging, user acceptance testing, and production release.

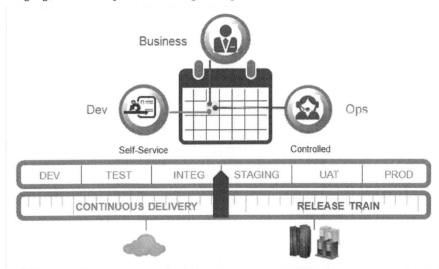

Source: Serena Software, Inc.

When you run continuous agile for the development team only, you still get benefits like:

- **Less stress.** You remove the stress that builds up before a release.
- A faster track for the most important fixes and enhancements
- A more scalable development team
- Lower meeting and management costs
- More time for developers and product owners to think

Measure results

If you do release software that only gets installed once per year, you probably find it frustrating that you only get feedback from users long after you work on something. Often, software companies don't even know what features get used. This puts you at a big disadvantage when trying to figure out how to improve the product. I STRONGLY encourage you to program your system to log feature usage, and optionally, send you the logs.

A walk on the wild side

Spinal Tap fans will be happy to know that there is an "11" on the CD Dial. You can release changes to production servers before you merge them to your mainline, and if they work, use the changes. This may involve inconveniences for your users, but it is an efficient test.

Remove Waterfall Stages

You will want to make a release map - a list of things that you do to plan, build, and release a change. This can have contain a lot of details about steps for review, testing, and deployment. Or, it can be very simple, and high level, like the diagram below. You will look for steps that you can shorten or remove.

Often, you will find that you have "waterfall" stages that are delaying each release. In the diagram below, we see that the "Program" stage is not very long. The programmers may even be using continuous integration and continuous delivery, so they can show changes quickly. However, the other stages of this process take longer.

After you have the release map, you can use four basic tactics to remove the waterfall stages. Think of it as SLAB - Skip, Lag, Automate, Blend.

Skip

Sometimes you get lucky and you can just skip a step. In the diagram below, we skip "Plan", and instead we let contributors pull tasks when they are ready.

Lag

We can Unblock! the release by lagging some tasks so that they come after one or more releases. Marketing and "launch" should always be lagged. Localization is often lagged. In the diagram below, we lag documentation and do it afterward, on a different schedule.

Automate

Automate as much as possible. You want to be able to finish a task as fast as you can run a script. In the diagram below, we apply automation to both testing and deployment.

Blend

You can blend one task with previous stages, so that it disappears as a waterfall stage and does not block anything. You can do manual testing while you are doing design and development, so that the QA person acts as a consultant, and not a gate.

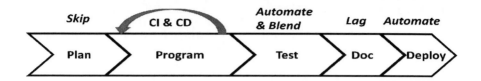

After applying all of these tactics, we might end up with a top-level release map that looks like this:

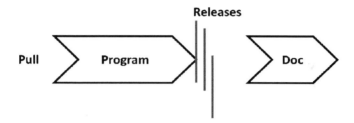

Release Strategies

My wife often calls me to announce that a major bank or airline web site she is using has gone down. Often they go down for weekend releases. She thinks their problems will make me feel better about the downtime that we have at Assembla, which is about one hour per quarter, or about one hour per 300 releases. But I think that tolerating any downtime is wimpy. There are a number of release strategies that those guys could use to avoid it. If you want to release more frequently, you have to be able to release without disrupting your users.

Beta releases

You can lower the risks of your continuous delivery process if you release to a subset of users and let them provide usability feedback and help you find bugs. These are your beta users. Most software companies inflict the beta version on their internal users. You should always be looking for ways to divide up your external user base and find beta users. You may want to test with free users. Some of your users will volunteer because they are innovators.

If you distributed installed software - including mobile clients - you will need beta users who will accept and download the beta releases.

- Automatically notify beta users when a new release is ready

- Send them release notes. You can automate the production of release notes by reading them from your development ticketing system. That will encourage users to try the new releases. You get extra credit for giving them a place to click to provide feedback.

I often tell my teams that we WILL release, but they can decide who to release to. If you partition your user base and add feature switches, you will have a lot of options and continuous delivery will not be stressful.

Automatic updates

Sometimes you can just run a script to update your software on customers' sites, if the software is designed to retrieve updates. Most consumer software works this way.

Sequential deployment to servers

High-volume online services can just update their banks of servers, one server at a time. That is what we do. Be sure that you can easily roll back.

Swap banks

If you have a complicated cluster, you can't update one server at a time. However, you can swap a whole cluster in seconds. Set up two banks of production servers. Run one in production. Deploy your new release to the second bank, and test it. Swap. Don't be a wimp about building new banks. It's cheaper to buy more hardware than to keep people waiting.

Swapping banks is the first thing I try with new customers that have complicated systems.

Service architecture

If you have a very complicated system you may be forced into a service architecture where you have many servers that call each other. Use the techniques described here to update only one component at a time. Even if your services are well tested, you will sometimes release something that causes an error. However, if you update one component at a time you will often find that the error only degrades a small number of features, while the rest of the system works fine. You can even program your service users to handle changes and errors.

Steps to Adopt Continuous Delivery

You can move to continuous delivery incrementally, in two simple steps.

1. Release more frequently
2. Improve

Questions for your team

- Why do we want to release more frequently?

- Who will you release to? You will need to find an audience and figure out how to get them using your releases.

- How will you measure the results? You want to find out if people are using the new stuff, and if it works for them.

- How frequently can you release?

Simple incentives, not culture change

You do not need extensive training and the dreaded "culture change." You can motivate your team to do the right thing with some simple incentives.

If you release frequently, your developers will stop ripping apart the software and breaking it. They will start using feature switches and other tactics to make incremental changes. You will not need to train them. They will figure it out.

If you require code review, you can get automated tests and compliance with coding standards. You can find people who believe the standards are important, and let them be the reviewers. You will not need an extensive set of policies, and training, and browbeating. You will not need to hire new people with a culture of test driven development. Only code that meets your standards will pass reviews. You can ask for tests, and you will get tests.

If you make developers decide when to release their changes, they will start to test more thoroughly and to automate tests and deployments. Remove the security blanket provided by your test phase and QA people. Make developers push the deploy button. You will get results.

If you make product managers and product owners responsible for unveil and measurement, they will start to work more intensively as "story owners" to make better features.

Phasing in

You can phase in continuous delivery with one team or service, and keep your existing batch release process for others. This will give you an opportunity to test some theories:

- Can you really choose between increased speed and increased quality?
- Can you do more experiments and get more feedback from your users?
- Do you have efficient testing and a good social framework for getting test coverage?
- Can you persuade your developers to take off the training wheels and release without QA approval?

Sample steps

You can build your continuous delivery capabilities in any order. The list below is a comfortable progression for a Scrum team that start by planning an iteration, testing a release candidate, and releasing in batches.

1) Maximize monitoring and reporting

The DevOps guys say "measure everything." You should maximize the amount of monitoring and reporting that you can get from the running software. You should get a good view of errors, usage volume, and feature usage patterns. This will give you confidence to release, because you will find and fix problems quickly. It will reduce your reliance on building automated tests. And, it will provide essential information for product management and improvement.

If you can measure some things about the development process, it will be easier to find and show improvements. Even very simple or crude measures will be useful. You can try to get a basic measure of velocity - counting points, or features, or tasks that get finished. How long does it actually take to go from an idea to a release? How frequently do people commit code? How long does it take to test the changes? How many bug reports are pending? How many times does a "finished" task get sent back for more work? Which changes actually result in an increase in usage?

Measurement is an easy first step because it doesn't disrupt anybody's existing way of working.

2) Scrumban, with no iteration plan

Throw out the iteration plan. Ask your developers to "pull" tasks when they are ready to work on them. At this stage, employ triage and test when you are ready to make a batch release. However, your developers will be working in a lean and continuous way. Remember, the goal of a lean system is to finish changes as quickly as possible. You do this by limiting the Work In Progress so that every task on the board is being worked on actively.

3) Automate build and deploy tasks

You will need automated build and deploy scripts as a foundation for repeatable testing and deployment. Aim for continuous improvement in your DevOps. If you have installed software or an installed client distribution, you should look for ways to automatically update the client software.

4) Use an Automated Test framework

You will need to add scripted tests to your code. This will be easy if you use one of the popular frameworks that include automated testing (for example, Ruby on Rails). Otherwise, look at our Test Types list and find some easy ways to layer in testing. For example, you will need to have good production monitoring, and in some cases this can substitute for other types of testing.

5) Code review and tests

Now you need to build automated tests. You need a social framework that motivates your team to build and maintain automated tests. You will get good results if you add code review, and have the reviewers who are enthusiastic about testing to ask for tests. You can use one of the review or branching code contribution patterns.

6) Continuous Integration and on-demand test systems

You need a fast and convenient way to run tests. You should put in a continuous integration system that will automate testing. You should also be able to build on-demand test systems for contributors who are working in a cascading or continuous process.

7) Changing role of QA

You need to unblock the approval of feature releases and get QA out of the way. Your QA people should be ready to serve as consultants for developers who ask for their help in making sure that changes do not create problems, and that features are actually useful.

If you have a good QA team, your developers may have become lazy and accustomed to throwing code over to QA without taking full responsibility for quality. At first, they will not believe that they can release directly. They will say it is too risky. At some point you will need to take off the training wheels and force them to ride the bike. If they must approve and do their own releases, they will figure out how to make them work reliably.

You will need to persuade developers to take responsibility for pushing out releases.

8) Kanban

Now your developers have test systems and QA support. They are ready to take responsibility for moving every change through to completion. You can move them to Kanban task management. They will "pull" a task, work on it, and finish it with a code release.

9) Move the CD Dial

Now you are ready to move the Continuous Delivery Dial and get closer and closer to releasing every change in real time. As you go faster, you might want to move your product owner role closer to a story owner role, so people in that role can be more closely involved in shaping features during development and unveil. You will want to improve your usage measurements so that you can monitor changes and respond. You may find that you can resolve more questions about product management through experiments. As you gain confidence in testing and assembling releases by pulling changes that are ready, you can expand your team.

Shortcuts

If you are feeling lucky, you can take some shortcuts that will save a lot of work.

My first suggestion is to skip the automated tests, and add them later. Use test layering. You might be able to rely on production monitoring instead. If you are running an online system, you should be monitoring the system for errors, and monitoring your users for their usage patterns. You can release to production, watch your errors and usage carefully, and roll back if there is a problem.

My second suggestion is to partition your user base so that you can release with less risk. Do you have users that get a free product? Are annoying? Are contributors? Give them the less-tested, frequent releases.

We will add more suggestions here as they come in from the field.

Continuous Coding

Four Patterns

This chapter contains four code contribution patterns for continuous delivery. You can pick a pattern, add test layers, and start releasing frequently.

Centralized

The centralized pattern is the traditional pattern popularized by Jez Humble. You put all of your changes together into one central code version, and continuously run automated tests on them. The goal is to integrate as early as possible, find problems as early as possible, and train your team to avoid them. It is easy to set up, and scales to support complex centralized build and test systems.

Distributed

The distributed pattern is used by many SaaS companies that want to release every change. Each change is tested in a separate branch, and then released before it hits problems from integration with other changes.

Review branch

The review branch system allows you to produce more reliable code from bigger teams, by testing and reviewing each change before it goes into a centralized shared version. This is a best practice.

MAXOS

The MAXOS pattern organizes continuous delivery of complex systems, which are built from multiple servers and services that communicate with each other. The team maintaining one service builds and releases changes, often using a review branch system. Before a service is promoted into production, it gets tested in a centralized continuous integration system to make sure that it works with the pre-release version of all of the other services.

Centralized

In centralized continuous integration, everyone contributes changes to a central trunk, master or mainline. A continuous integration system is continually running automated tests on this version. The goal is to find and fix problems as early as possible. Developers have incentives to avoid "breaking the build" and make sure that the mainline is always at release quality.

Centralized CI/CD

Contributor Commits – "as early as possible" to find problems

Continuous Integration tests

Fail - alarm   Pass

Release Candidate Test System   Release

QA Testing

Key concepts of continuous delivery include:

- **Automated tests**. You need enough automated tests to tell you immediately if something is broken. You run them frequently.

- **Developer responsibility**. It is the responsibility of the developers to make sure that their code doesn't break anything. They can't just throw it over to QA and wait for bug reports. The centralized system enforces an extreme form of developer responsibility by sending an alarm if the system does not build, or if tests fail. This "broken build" demands attention. In some shops, it triggers sirens and flashing lights.

- **Feature switches**. Developers are constantly releasing code for new features, but they need to hide features that aren't ready. They put switches in the code to hide changes that aren't officially released or "unveiled."

Advantages

Centralization is efficient. There is one test system, which is important if your test environment is complicated. You don't have to move code between multiple versions. You know where to go for manual testing.

Because of its efficiency, this is a great pattern for small teams. It is also a good pattern for systems that have very complicated test environments.

This approach relies on the principle of "as early as possible" integration and discovery of problems. People are committing frequently, tests run frequently, and conflicts between changes are discovered quickly. This minimizes the amount of wasted programming effort and improves efficiency.

Centralized continuous integration works well with Subversion, where it is called "active trunk." Subversion does a good job of synchronizing developers onto a single stream.

Disadvantages

Centralized continuous delivery doesn't scale very well if you have many contributors, many new contributors, or distributed teams. The more changes that you put into the shared version, the more often you will have a "broken build" that doesn't work, or possibly doesn't even compile.

As you add distributed contributors, the process becomes more stressful. To avoid delaying everyone else, every contributor has to be alert to broken tests and broken builds and fix them immediately, regardless of time zone. This puts extra stress on distributed team members and gives them responsibilities after the end of their workday. Jez Humble is an advocate of the centralized approach, but he doesn't recommend it for truly distributed teams.

You can't release every change. Whenever you put two changes together for "early as possible" integration, you expect to find problems. The software is not releasable until you have tested for the possibility of new problems.

The fix: Test and review

Centralized continuous delivery is well suited to a two-week release cycle that includes user acceptance testing and batched releases. With this release cycle it often becomes a continuous integration system, and not a continuous delivery system. But if you want to release every day, or release every change, you may decide make a major leap from "as early as possible" integration to "as late as possible."

You can eliminate almost all of these disadvantages and go to continuous release if you test and review incoming commits. We will discuss this below.

Distributed

Some modern online services have hundreds or thousands of developers and release once, twice or 50 times per day. They do it with a distributed continuous process in which each change gets tested and released independently.

You cannot guarantee that your change will work with all the other changes produced by a big group of developers. To solve this problem, distributed continuous delivery leaps from "as early as possible" integration to "as late as possible" integration. With "as late as possible" integration you test each change with a recent production version of the code before you merge it with the other candidate changes.

Distributed Continuous Delivery

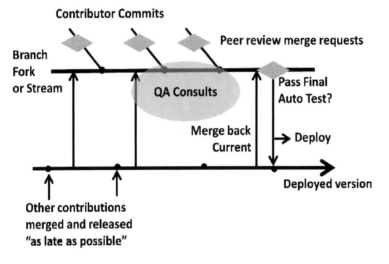

Here is how it works:

1. As an individual or team committer, you put changes into your own branch or fork.

2. For testing, you merge the production version to your change branch. This gives you a release candidate on your workstation for testing. Git has a special operation called "rebase" that helps you merge the target version, and then batches your changes up into a single package for delivery.

3. Your development organization takes advantage of cloud computing to give every contributor an on-demand test

environment. QA acts in a consulting role, looking at your test environment if you need help verifying that changes are good and desirable.

4. You do a final test and deploy. This is highly automated. You need to make sure that your change works with the most recent release, so you do a final update with automated tests. If this passes, the system will deploy.

Advantages

With the distributed process, you can release every change immediately. This provides a competitive advantage for online applications and service providers. The continuous release process also reduces stress by getting fixes out more quickly, and by allowing big changes to be completed in the minimum time needed to actually do the work. Finally, the distributed continuous delivery process can include a large number of contributors distributed in multiple time zones.

Disadvantages

With distributed continuous delivery, test environments are more complicated. Setting up multiple test environments creates a bigger workload for DevOps. Developers are responsible for maintaining versions and shepherding changes through tests. They need to know more about the test environments.

You may not have time to release all of your changes. It takes time to run the final test and deploy, because automated tests take time. Changes are tested and released sequentially. Tests for each change need to wait for tests to be completed on previous changes. If you have a lot of contributors, you may not have time to release all of their changes. To address this issue you can make a faster pre-release "smoke test," or you can cascade and batch up the changes.

Critics often observe that developers using this approach tend to work a long time on their branches and then cause integration problems when they merge big batches of code. Finding problems in these big batches of code is difficult. If you use distributed continuous delivery you should:

- Frequently "merge back" from the production version to your development version. If you do frequent integration and test in your development version, you will find and fix problems before you merge "forward" into the production version.

- Release changes as frequently as possible. When you release smaller amounts of code, you have fewer places to look for problems and you will find them faster.

Multiple test environments

You will want to have multiple test environments, so that you can test each change separately. Testers will act as consultants, helping when developers ask them to look at a specific test system. Building and maintaining these test environments takes some work. However, you can use the miracle of cloud computing and versioned configurations to deliver test environments on-demand, allowing you to work with an unlimited number of contributors.

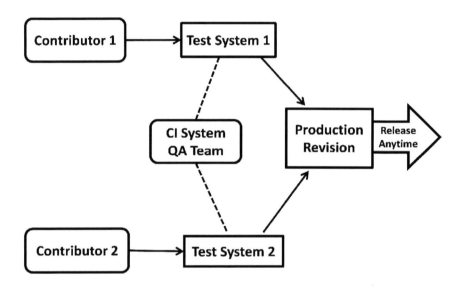

Branch Review

Scaling with branch review

You can improve the scalability of a centralized continuous delivery process by adding code review. This gives you some of the simplicity of the centralized process, with some of the scalability of the distributed or continuous release process.

We like a review process where every contribution aimed at the master branch goes into a temporary branch, where it can be tested and reviewed by automated tests and by other developers.

Contributor Commits

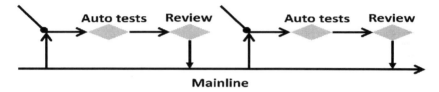

Mainline

Adding change review to a centralized continuous delivery process increases the quality and stability of the target branch because it:

- Gives you a convenient place to put "pre-commit" automated tests, so that your automated test system can reject changes that don't pass before they are merged with the mainline.

- Saves reviewer time, because reviewers do not look at code until it at least passes the automated tests.

- Helps you bring in new contributors through reviews and comments.

- Allows you to have a much larger number of contributors without breaking the build.

- Helps you build your suite of automated tests, because your reviewers can ask contributors for automated tests.

Merge request implementation

In one implementation of this workflow, a contributor submits a "merge request" or "pull request." Automated test systems and reviewers can pull the change and test it before agreeing to merge it.

Temporary branch implementation

In systems like Gerrit, contributed changes automatically go into a temporary branch. The built-in workflow will run tests, collect reviews, merge the change, and throw away the branch. This process tends to be more centralized and unified, because contributors start from the shared branch and they do not have to maintain their own branch or fork.

Assembla implements both workflows, merge request and temporary branch.

Pre-flight testing and review

If you do not want to make a lot of branches, or if you have a code repository that does not support lightweight branches, you can do pre-flight testing and review by having a second system that looks at changes before they get committed to the shared repository. This is called "pre-flight" testing. For example, Electric Cloud makes a system which can overlay pre-flight testing on various code repositories.

Distributed starts to look like centralized

Just as a centralized continuous delivery process can take on elements of distributed processes, so too can a distributed process evolve to resemble centralized processes.

In a distributed continuous delivery process there is an incentive to release frequent, small changes. Why? Because small changes are easier to debug. If you discover a problem, you only have to look through a small amount of changed code to find it and fix it. When problems show up in a large release, they are harder to fix and they create more stress.

Because of this incentive, distributed continuous delivery teams often move over time to frequent, small releases, with a mainline that is constantly updated. This mainline version will look similar to a single centralized version.

Matrix of Services

Matrix of Services, which I will call MAXOS, is a way to organize continuous delivery of large systems. To start, big applications are divided into smaller services. For example, one service might render a Web page, and call a different service to get information about a product. Each development team maintains a small number of services, and releases changes when changes are ready. Amazon, which has thousands of services, will release a change about once every 11 seconds, adding up to about 8000 changes per day.

Matrix of Services

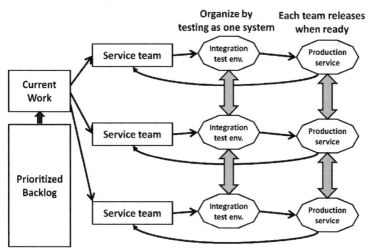

Feedback on speed, errors, usage, and requests

Service changes: Branch review, then centralized CI

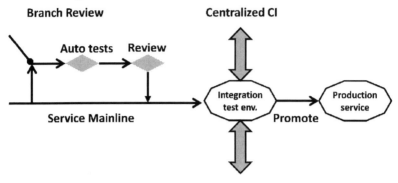

1) Change a service

Each team makes changes to the services they are responsible for. Often, they use a branch review process to contribute changes that are promoted to the staging or integration version.

The MAXOS system emphasizes developer responsibility. Programmers lead each team, and the team takes complete responsibility for design, programming, testing, and release of some set of services. There are often so many different services that the operations team cannot track and configure all of them. To compensate, developers take some responsibility for operations, monitoring performance, responding to alerts, and pushing fixes.

2) Test services together

The most recent version of each service runs in a centralized continuous integration system. Automated tests exercise the calls between services to make sure that the integrated system works correctly. This system is often radically centralized, with one test system for thousands of services. Having only one test system makes it possible to maintain a complex and complete test environment.

If a service passes all of its tests in the integration environment, its team can promote it into production. If it doesn't pass the centralized tests, then the team can track down the calls that failed and work with other teams to fix any integration problems. The centralized continuous integration system uncovers dependency problems, and greatly simplifies the task of organizing a big project with interrelated parts.

MAXOS allows mere humans to build computer systems at a new level of scale, dubbed "Web-scale IT." I will write more about the implications of MAXOS in the chapter on "Continuous Enterprise."

Continuous Stories

Themes

Be yourself, innovate, and have fun releasing more frequently. These stories show that you don't need to follow a formula.

This section contains stories about teams releasing frequently. All of the stories are different, and they are in different formats. If you do large scale software development or build a product, I recommend that you read all of these stories and consider the various approaches. If you do smaller projects for clients, you can skip to "Working with Clients" and get some useful hints.

You may eventually get sucked in by some common trends and themes. Here are a few things that came up frequently.

Many virtual servers. Continuous delivery takes a LOT of servers. Don't fight it. Automation is good. Servers are cheaper than people.

Distributed teams. Your teams will spread out and manage their own time. Help them become happy.

Programmer responsibility. Programmers incrementally take control of the release schedule, testing, and operations.

Team restructuring. We found that teams took complete responsibility for one or more front-end services, plus any related back-end services. QA professionals were blended with programming teams. Some organizations kept scrum-style multifunctional teams, but run by programming tech leads, and some went directly to a core of programmers, plus other functions (design, db, test, ops) as consultants.

Inadequate use of data. We have a lot of data about how people use software, lying around in logs, and even in reports and dashboards, but we aren't using it. Only the best organizations are using all of their data to figure out what features and changes have high impact, and invest in those.

Service architecture and MAXOS organization. As I collected these stories, I came to an unexpected discovery. The best organizations have traveled on different journeys, with different vocabulary, and different tools, but they have arrived at a similar technique, which I call Matrix of Services or MAXOS. They are dividing their apps and infrastructure into many Web services. They run continuous delivery for each service. They use automated testing to continuously integrate the most recent version of each service. This technique ingeniously replaces the very difficult job of project management, dependency planning, and scrum of scrums with continuous integration - that is, with a machine. I've made notes about this technique in the stories about Google, HubSpot, and Edmunds.

Centralized Continuous Delivery at Google

Google runs an extreme form of centralized continuous delivery. According to a report at an event in 2013, they have 15,000 developers working on 5,000 projects, committing to ONE current version of the code. Their single source code tree contains 100M lines of code. They run continuous tests on the "head," or most recent version, and when it looks good, they release it.

Their technique is successful. Google runs many of the Web's biggest services, and runs them reliably. Their products adapt quickly, and in some cases they can go from idea to release in 48 hours.

Google's approach is in large part determined by the way that they share code and Web services between projects. An engineer reports that developers "can make changes to kernel, Gmail, and other Google apps in the same changelist." This ability to make changes across the entire system allows engineers to make structural changes without a lot of organizational work and delay. However, it also means that they must run a centralized process with a single version of the test system. They can't run test systems for one component. They need to be able to test every service for any changelist. The Google test system is continuously compiling, caching and deploying all of the components required to run a test of the most recent code version - while running 100M test cases per day.

Many of the other aspects of development at Google fall out naturally from the decision to build and test one integrated system.

They require code review. If you are running test and deploy from one shared version of the code, you want a review before the code is committed.

They typically work in small, co-located teams. Google is a sprawling business, but most of the programming work is done by groups of 3-4 people who work together in one office. This makes it easy to get a code review. Each team has a tech lead. They don't use non-technical project managers and Agile functionaries. When your teams rely on code review and code deploy, you use tech leads who speak code.

They have a "test engineering" group to build and run the testing systems. The test engineering group is about 15% of the total developer base, which seems quite efficient to me.

The test engineers think a lot about "social engineering": creating a social framework that motivates developers to fix bugs and write tests for good test coverage. They keep leaderboards that report on bug counts and test coverage by developer.

Google uses a code management system that is based on Perforce. Perforce handles very large code repositories containing multiple projects. It also has a structure called a "changelist" that holds changes which are ready for review.

Scaling the organization with services, and continuous integration

Google was able to grow to a huge scale and an extremely complex environment because:

- They divided their vast Internet system into thousands of "services."

- Developers make frequent changes to services. However, before they release a change, they test it with the most recent version of all the other services. If a test script finds problems in the interactions between two services, it can tell developers who to contact to resolve the problems.

Google is using continuous integration to replace other, more complicated forms of planning. For decades, large-scale IT projects crashed and burned because project planners could not figure out all of the dependencies. Google can manage at an even bigger scale because they replaced this project management with a testing machine that continuously finds dependency problems. It is a fantastic management innovation, which I will describe in the chapter on "Continuous Enterprise."

Distributed Continuous Delivery at Assembla

Assembla uses a distributed continuous delivery system in which developers use multiple code branches and test systems. This is a common configuration for Web and SaaS shops, because it allows them to release every change directly to production servers.

Distributed teams. Assembla also uses fully distributed teams, with 25 people spread across 10 different countries. This is also a common configuration for modern capital efficient startups. We recruit wherever we can find the best people. We use two-week trials where we throw the new candidate in with an experienced tech lead. Developers have organized themselves into 3-person feature teams, which improves online collaboration, and gives them two buddies to to ask for code review when they need it. Each team has a tech lead who can call on a specialist for graphic design or QA.

Kanban task management. We have found that development teams can work effectively off an online Cardwall. They pull their own work. We do frequent reviews of the amount of work in progress to keep it manageable.

Automated testing with on-demand test systems. Over the course of a year we invested in test infrastructure. We currently use cloud computing to start complete test instances of our system for every merge request. This allows us to run automated tests and to hand off a working system to a QA person and story owner for manual testing and review.

Story-owner product management and user experience design. One person is responsible for constructing the story, for design, for "unveiling" the feature, and for follow-up and usage statistics.

Git-based code management with short-lived feature branches and required code review. We use the **distributed continuous delivery** pattern (described in this book), which allows us to release each change after it has been tested in its own test environment. We started with feature bigger teams that shared a development branch and a test server. However, we found that a problem with one change would block other changes from being released. Changes would accumulate for several days, and snowball into large releases that were difficult to debug. So we looked for ways to move each change through the system independently.

CTO Michael Chletsos explains:

The real decision that we made was to make one developer responsible for a change, from development, through testing, to production monitoring. We went through a series of steps to "unblock" developers:

- We added on-off switches to significant changes, so that developers can release them without being blocked by story owners. Story owners can control the "unveil" of a feature after it is on a production system.

- We provided on-demand test systems. Each change gets its own test system that runs automated tests, and also shows the change to story owners and QA. At Assembla, which is a small company, we use the magic of cloud computing to run up to 60 test servers at one time.

- Code review is required. This creates a blocking step, but we need it because it gives us a place to ask for test scripts that feed the automated test process. Manual QA is not required, but we put in some features to make it easier. For example, when a merge request gets deployed to an on-demand test server, we put a clickable link to that server on the related feature ticket.

- Developers trigger the deployment of a change. Developers can deploy whenever they want. They tell a bot to deploy a merge request.

- The Master version is always deployable because it is always deployed. The bot merges to master, runs an automated smoke test, and deploys. Test must take less than five minutes.

- We opened up monitoring so that developers can see all of the details of load and usage on the production servers.

Technical details: Story of a code change at Assembla

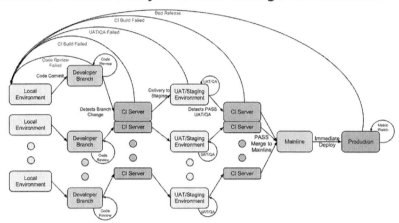

Here is the story of how a code change is handled at Assembla:

1. Dev commits a code change

2. The code commit is referenced on a ticket

3. A Merge Request (MR) is created by the developer (this could be a push to the master with a protected branch)

4. Jenkins picks up the change based on a webhook fired when the merge request was created

5. Jenkins, developers, and QA do several things in parallel:

   - A new staging environment is created with the current code plus the changeset, and the ticket is updated to notify QA that the staging environment is ready.
   - All integration tests are performed on the current production release plus the changeset; when it is completed the merge request receives a vote of +1 or -1.
   - QA tests the staging environment.
   - Developers perform a code review.

6. When tests are completed and the merge request receives a vote of +1 from development, Jenkins and QA, the developer asks the bot to deploy the merge request in a chat:

   - 6a. The bot merges the merge request to the master.
   - 6b. The bot deploys the change out to production.
   - 6c. The bot writes a link into the ticket that shows where the changeset is being deployed

7. The change is deployed to the production environment.

HubSpot Transformed

HubSpot transformed their aging, monolithic SaaS application into a vibrant matrix of 200 services, and they transformed their stressful release cycles into a stream of 100 change releases per day. Along the way, they have grown from a promising startup to an IPO-bound juggernaut. A few years ago I had dinner with both employees, founders Dharmesh Shah and Brian Halligan. On a recent visit, I found 600 people in their office.

HubSpot popularized the idea of using content and shared expertise to bring prospects to a Web site, eager to learn and to buy. They contrast this "inbound marketing" with the old outbound marketing, which sends messages out to unwilling victims, and is mostly ignored. Their SaaS product provides a complete suite of tools for small and medium-sized businesses to blog, publish, optimize, inform, and collect leads. They have used inbound marketing with some flair. The rapid growth of their SaaS service has been propelled by their Website Grader site, excellent blogging about online marketing, and other contributions.

I have used their blogging tool from its first launch, and I can testify that it's a useful service. However, in those early days, their marketing and ideas were noticeably better than the product. Even after four years of development, the software lacked some simple features like a reliable "remember me" login, and it was looking old. They decided to rebuild it with a new service architecture and new development teams.

Building all new code to upgrade an existing product is a famously risky maneuver. I once lost $6 million on such a bet. However, the new HubSpot product quickly surpassed the old product, and is now adding features and invading related categories at a rate that makes it a serious threat to competing vendors. This transformation is impressive because of its speed - it took about one year - and the fact that they were able to do it incrementally by ramping up new services and steadily ramping down the effort on the old codebase.

I interviewed Elias Torres to dive into their development process. I found him in HubSpot's bustling headquarters, where small teams worked under monitors showing real time performance and usage statistics.

HubSpot runs a pure form of MAXOS with programmer-driven service teams.

Teams and process

HubSpot teams have a tech lead and two engineers. There are about 20 teams maintaining about 200 services, so each team has about 10 services. There are about 30 other members of the development team doing design and product management. The small teams are organized into "clusters" which support complete products, or categories like mobile. Each cluster has a UX designer and a product manager.

To change a service, a developer submits a merge request. A colleague reviews it and merges it into the Git master branch for the service. A QA system automatically pulls the current master branch for each service and runs automated tests. Currently, the QA system is testing code from 500 different repositories that contain code and configurations. Integration tests include Selenium functional tests, and tests are added for bugs that customers have found. If the integration tests look good, the developer runs a command to deploy the modified service to production servers.

Developer responsibility and self-organization

In order to make sure that every service gets expert attention through its complete life cycle, HubSpot gives developers a lot of responsibility. HubSpot development teams are responsible for design, programming, testing, release, monitoring, and responding to production problems. They can call on their cluster UX experts for design. They have no full time QA professionals. They have a custom monitoring and alert system that alerts members of a specific development team if there is a problem.

HubSpot teams are in many ways self-organizing, because they get so much monitoring and information about the services they own. The can see load, speed, and errors on a real time dashboard. They read customer questions and complaints submitted to the HubSpot knowledge base. These various inputs are combined into a "quality score." If they release a lot of new changes, the quality score is likely to decline. When it goes below a threshold, the team focuses its effort on improving quality. So, the process balances itself.

Tooling

Elias says "it's all about empowering the team to do as much as possible, as quickly as possible. Tools provide guard rails." HubSpot operations provides their service teams with proprietary tools for configuration, release, and monitoring. All of their services and servers (2000 servers on Amazon) are mapped in a dashboard with red/yellow/green indicators.

They have sophisticated tooling for feature switches, which they call "gates." There is a centralized gate manager with a Web based editor. Developers and product managers can turn on features for a complete system (QA or production) or for individual customers. Gates allow them to do usability testing with selected customers before they unveil.

To do

Elias says that he wants to add some layers of testing, including an automated unit test that run before human review, completing the branch review process. With this move, HubSpot will have a complete best-of-breed MAXOS process.

Edmunds Accelerates

I'd like to thank our friends at Perforce for putting us in touch with Edmunds.com, one of their customers and an excellent example of a company that has used the principles of Continuous Agile to strengthen its competitive position.

Edmunds.com provides authentic automotive information and a high-quality online shopping experience to automotive consumers, delivering the scoop about shiny new automobiles to more than 13 million unique monthly visitors. They also drive hundreds of mobile apps through their external API. They stay in top gear by releasing several times per day, and by planning product initiatives on timelines as short as weeks.

According to Ajit Zadgaonkar, Senior Director of Software Engineering, It wasn't always this way. He remembers when the business was dependent on annual plans with a quarterly release schedule. MS Project plans caused them to "lock down" on finishing features that weren't needed. Engineers were frustrated because they had to wait 90 days or more to see their changes deployed. Sometimes their innovations never made it to release.

By moving to more frequent release schedules, the engineers can see successes every day, and quickly make adjustments when new features are not as popular as expected. Ajit says that the teams have lost their fear of failure. The business has more appetite for innovation and experimentation.

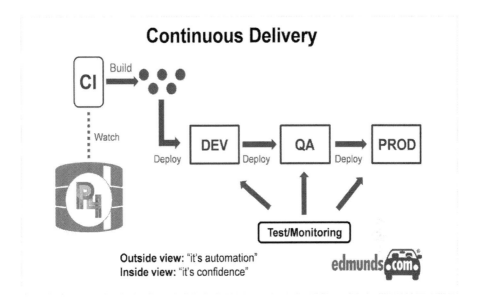

Edmunds illustrates how the themes of Continuous Agile link together, sometimes without conscious planning.

Incremental improvements

Edmunds improved their release frequency incrementally: from every 3 months, to every month, to several times a day. They consolidated all of their code changes onto one release branch, and added feature flags to hide the features that weren't ready. They re-engineered their 40 person traditional QA team into a software engineering team. They enhanced the traditional software developer role to a well-rounded "software Engineer" with software development, testing and "Operationability" responsibilities - the big difference being that quality and critical software engineering functions were built into the role rather than being bolted on. They added test layers to build confidence. They provided access and visibility into production monitoring dashboards.

"Results only" teams

Before they started releasing more frequently, Edmunds moved to a distributed team structure. The whole team officially works out of their office in lovely Santa Monica. However, they aren't required to be in the office at any specific times, and often they aren't. Ajit says that, although it took two years to implement the new "results only work environment" across the entire company, it substantially improved both happiness and velocity.

Service architecture

Moving to a service architecture was a key step. Edmunds broke their monolithic Java app into 36 different services. Each service can be tested and deployed separately. A development team is typically totally responsible for one front-end service or feature, and has shared responsibility for all of the back-end services that it consumes.

Like HubSpot, Edmunds is using the "matrix of services" architecture and process. Each service team makes changes whenever they are ready, with an understanding that their changes will be backwards compatible, and will not break other services. Each service goes through centralized compatibility tests and regression tests to ensure it works with the most recent development version of the other services.

The promotion process uses a centralized continuous delivery approach. Programmers commit code to one Perforce Versioning Engine branch. The most recent code is compiled into a Java file and passed into a Nexus repository for testing and promotion. A stable service gets promoted into the "blue" bank of servers and switched on, and then the development team monitors the results.

Test layering

The Edmunds release process is a beautiful example of test layering. In this diagram they show how a change goes through eight layers of automated testing.

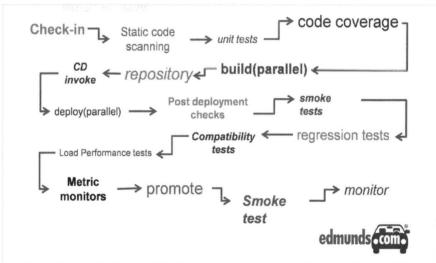

Edmunds doesn't worry about having high "test coverage" at every layer. Instead, when they see a problem, they write a test to prevent it from happening again and select the best place to put the test.

Edmunds uses the bank-switching release method for their Web site. At any given time, they have a "green" active bank and a "blue" inactive bank. After they update and test the blue bank, they switch over to the new code on the blue bank. If they see any problems, they can switch back.

 Ajit emphasizes that it is important to provide developers with fast testing and feedback so they can address problems immediately. All of their automated test processes are optimized and parallelized across multiple machines. Final production tests must run in less than 8 minutes. This process requires a lot of servers. They run their test layering with a development bank, a staging bank, and additional servers for build, test, and monitoring. To handle all of this they are currently using a hybrid public and private cloud architecture.

Data-driven product management

Edmunds team members can get the data they need to make good decisions. Everyone in the company has access to key success factors, A/B test results, and the health of various environments and features. Ajit suspects this may be just the start. As with many organizations, the next step for Edmunds is to use real time data streams of continuous feedback to help them identify areas of improvement, and to channel energy to focus on high impact issues.

oDesk Beyond Scrum

oDesk is the world's largest online marketplace for contract talent. Their Web site allows businesses to find, hire, manage, and pay talented freelancers from around the world. oDesk posts over 1.5 million jobs a year in categories like web development, software development, networking and information systems, and design and multimedia.

oDesk provides an example for organizations who have Scrum-style, multifunctional teams and want to Unblock! for more capacity and more frequent releases.

Geographically expansive

oDesk has been able to dramatically expand their development capacity by utilizing a geographically distributed organization. By recruiting and managing geographically distributed teams, they bypass the intense competition for talent around their home location in Silicon Valley. The oDesk development team now has about 200 people, including about 150 programmers, 15 project managers, 5 designers, 30 test engineers, 10 devops, and 10 database specialists. Seventy-five percent of these people work from remote locations.

It's not easy for remote engineers to understand a system as big as oDesk. They need to have great problem solving skills, because they are physically isolated and working alone. They need great communication skills, because communicating with online chats and hangouts is harder than with a white board. They also need to be technically very independent.

oDesk's recruiting process reflects these requirements. They hire only the top developers available on oDesk, and only after extensive testing. Candidates spend 1-2 weeks in a "bootcamp," where they work on simple changes and learn coding practices and technical architecture. They don't get access to the entire code base until they are experienced.

Development process

To release more frequently, oDesk made a few specific changes.

Organize by feature: Previously, teams were organized by layer, working on front end, services, or the database. This required a lot of communication and (online) meetings to coordinate a complete change across all layers. The new teams own relatively well defined and self-contained areas of the product, such as freelancer search, client onboarding, or the payment platform.

oDesk currently has 25 teams. Each team has a PM (product manager or product owner), and many PMs work on two or three teams at a time. Each team also has an architect who has a fairly rich role, in that he is at the same time the scrum master, the engineering manager, the architect and the lead dev. An architect manages between three and ten developers. A typical team will include three PHP developers (our front end), one html/css/javascript developer, one Java developer (our middle layer), and one test engineer. The bigger teams tend to informally break themselves out as multiple smaller teams.

Continuous integration: All commits trigger a CI run which completes all unit tests in about 10 minutes.

Teams are responsible for testing and operations: oDesk has kept a small centralized QA organization for overall regression testing and test framework development, but most of QA is in the teams. Development teams are also taking more responsibility for operational roles: DevOps and SiteOps.

Feature flags: Developers are encouraged to commit to the master branch very frequently, and to use feature flags to control the visibility of their features.

Q&A

I interviewed the oDesk VP of Products, Stephane Kasriel, to find out how oDesk adapted to more frequent releases.

How do you feel about working with a geographically distributed team?

We "eat our own dog food." Seventy-five percent of the team is remote (oDesk freelancers), and mostly they are remote from each other too, working from home. We have three small offices, but most of the teams don't work from there.

This is awesome in many ways. We have access to amazing talent that other Bay Area-based startups are ignoring, and we are able to attract and retain people for a long time. We hired 40 developers in the last six months; I don't think that many startups are able to do that. Our developers are heavy users of our web site, which allows everyone to think about ways to improve the product constantly.

There are downsides. Obviously it's just harder to collaborate remotely. While remote teams are aware that they need to adapt their schedules to maximize overlap in time zones, it's still not close to 100%. All in all, we think that our productivity is about 20% less than it would be if we had the same developers locally. But of course that's a very theoretical exercise, because we don't think we could have that number of talented people here given the incredible level of competition in our neighborhood.

Did you change testing? Did you add test layers?

Yes, this was a huge part of it. We have always had a unit testing system and a functional testing system. However, they weren't essential. Unit tests had low coverage. They could be broken on master for days at a time, even weeks in some cases.

Functional tests were owned by a test automation team that was completely isolated from the dev team. The architects would tell the manual QA team what the features were about. The manual QA team would write test case documents and execute them manually. Then they would tell the test automation team to automate a subset of those tests. As a result, coverage was extremely low, and the tests broke all the time. When the product changed, it took days for the automation team to know how to change their tests. Everyone was dissatisfied with how the interaction worked.

Now, developers are fully accountable for unit tests. Many teams have switched to test driven development. But even for the ones that haven't, there's a strict requirement that you cannot merge code that doesn't pass all unit tests. We've moved most of the test automation engineers into the Agile teams, under the direct supervision of the team lead. We've also radically rebalanced the QA organization from having a large manual team and a small automation team, to having a small manual team and a large automation team.

We have also dramatically improved the speed of execution of the tests. We profiled the testing code and improved it. We switched from browsers to PhantomJS, parallelized, and added hardware. We can run all of the tests in a few hours instead of holding code for a full week before release. We've become comfortable releasing a lot more often because we are much more confident that our unit and functional tests cover the important use cases and that nothing dramatic will happen when we release.

Did you change the code review process?

We moved from posting code on a review board to active pull requests. But probably more importantly, we've moved from big commits and long running branches, which are a complete nightmare, to frequent commits and frequent merges.

Did you add to your feature flag system?

We created the feature flag system for the purpose of switching to Continuous Delivery. We never needed it before, because developers would primarily merge when features were complete. Feature flags are not perfect; for example, nobody is excited about having to clean up the dead code after feature flags are permanently turned on. But feature flags have enabled us to move to a "branch by abstraction" model, which really helps reduce the risk in each release.

Did you change any roles? For example, did you move any responsibility for approval from testers to developers? We find that this almost always happens in a continuous process. How did you change the role of developers, test, and devops?

Yes. Responsibility moved from a centralized QA organization, which still exists but is 10% of its former size, to each team lead. We are not yet at the point where every team has its own independently deployable assembly. At least half of the teams still contribute to a single deployment artifact, so there is still overall management oversight, but it's relatively lightweight. Team leads sign off in a permanent skype chat, and then we release the code.

It's a big group. How do you manage dependencies and communication between teams?

At the beginning of the year we publish a 10 page product and technical strategy document, which guides us throughout the year. Every six weeks, each Agile team presents progress and plans to our engineering directors. The directors can help them identify and solve dependencies. We have a group of eight directors that meets weekly to make significant architectural decisions.

We're trying to remove dependencies by verticalizing the stack. It's an ongoing process and one that takes months to complete. Of course, even in a verticalized environment, there are always features that cross boundaries. When the crossing is small and the team is knowledgeable, the team changes the other team's code and gets it reviewed and approved through pull requests. When the crossing is higher, the teams synchronize during their sprint planning meeting, and dependent tasks are prioritized by the corresponding teams. When prioritization issues occur, they get escalated and I make a decision with our directors. Communication happens mostly between the architects and team leads, a relatively contained group of about 40 engineers. We have a weekly 90-minute meeting, which happens over Google Hangout and a phone line.

Are you dividing your code into separate services?

We're still in the process. The idea is to go from three fairly entangled horizontal tiers (front, middle, and database) to verticalized stacks. One of the main challenges in doing so is to isolate reusable classes and functions into packages, and then rewrite the non-reusable code into independent repositories that leverage those shared packages.

Mobile Apps

Mobile developers are designing a user experience. They need the power of Continuous Agile to work with users from day to day and to mold the look and feel of their applications. However, they also face three challenges:

- They are building a server and a client. The client must be distributed to the mobile devices.

- Appstore vendors add delays in distribution of two days to three weeks.

- They are designing software to run on multiple devices and form factors.

Luca Milanesio of LMIT Software explains how to use Jenkins and Android for continuous delivery of a mobile user experience

Moving towards Kanban and Continuous Delivery on Mobile

Most of the software development community is unleashing the power of Agile by moving away from SCRUM sprint-based planning to more Agile Kanban-style feature development. This features a new methodology promoted by the DevOps Movement (http://en.wikipedia.org/wiki/DevOps) and implemented by marrying continuous integration methodology with automated deployment. This is now known as continuous deployment.

However, the mobile applications market is struggling with a flashback to "waterfall" planning methods imposed by mobile platform owners.

Continuous deployment makes sense for the cloud backend development which powers the RESTFul API used by mobile apps. But does it make sense to extend it to the client layer as well ?

Releasing without Continuous Delivery

One solution to the problem is to isolate the mobile clients from the backend cloud deployments, keeping them as much as possible in different silos with a set of APIs between them.

In this environment, new ideas go into the backlog, changes are done in both client and backend layers, and features are developed and tested in a few days, Kanban-style.

However, continuous delivery is not implemented. The back end is deployed to the cloud in real time after the build. But deploying the updated mobile client takes longer. The packaging of the mobile client has been completed, but distribution is just starting. The mobile distribution channel typically takes from two to five days. And after distribution is completed, before you can get feedback, you still need to allow time for real users to install and discover the new features.

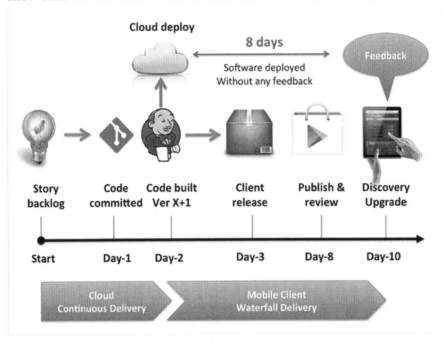

This issue is illustrated in the diagram below.

The development team starts work on the next feature on Day 3. However, no feedback is available until Day 10. Feature development starts to overlap between releases and block new releases. Because of this, delays in delivering the mobile app impact the entire Kanban cycle.

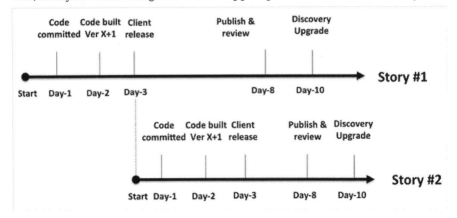

Releasing with Continuous Delivery

In our continuous delivery system, the client and backend are built and delivered at the same time. Selected users see the completed feature and provide feedback before it is delivered to the official distribution channel.

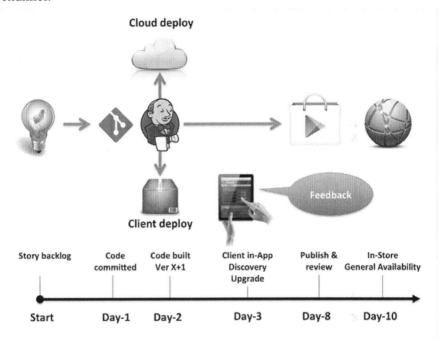

Bringing the Kanban methodology to Mobile

With Kanban it is key to reduce the size of each deployment by limiting the size of your work-in-progress queue (which determines the scope of the new release). Your team will finish a task before moving to the next task.

To achieve high velocity you must reduce the time required to get new software to mobile devices:

1. Clients need to find alternate ways to install the software in addition to the official mobile platform distribution channel.

2. App users need to be informed early on about the availability of a new software release, and should be able to install it seamlessly.

3. App users must have visibility into what has changed in the

new software. Provide them with release notes.

When dealing with mobile applications it is key that everybody is involved in providing feedback on the application itself. It is not uncommon to have early alphas installed on every developer's smartphone in order to have someone using the app on a daily basis, even in its early stages.

We like to give our users visibility into all the tickets that are in the WIP queue, and even allow them to comment with a simple "Like it, seems cool !" or "Please don't do that, would kill my daily experience #!$@#!".

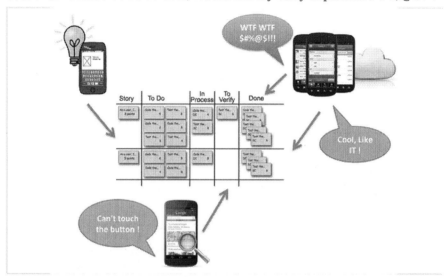

The most important concept behind Agile is the "fast feedback loop." The sooner you get feedback on a feature, either positive or negative, the better your choice of the next task to make the user happy. Fast is often a synonym of "easy" and "automatic." If you make something easy for people, they will do it more often.

Auto-assign feedback to stories

Users of your mobile application should see the stories that are implemented in a new software release. They can look at the affected features and use cases and provide feedback. Feedback should be automatically attached to the original story, so that it immediately goes to the correct developer.

Client Ver. X   One-tap upgrade   Client Ver. Y

Imagine that you introduce a new feature to send instant messages to other users. If you give users access to a full description of this feature, you will have the chance to get feedback while they are still on your app. When they have completed a successful flow for the feature, ask them for positive or negative feedback and a short explanation.

Some users will not be interested in the new feature and will continue to use the app as before. For these users, anomalies introduced by the new release can be classified as "side-regressions." Negative feedback from these users can identify features that are impacting the overall stability of your product.

Distribute Clients Directly from Continuous Integration

There are many tools to provide ad-hoc over-the-air (OTA) software distribution and to collect feedback from customers (i.e. Zubhium, TestFlight, Hockeyapp, Apphance). However, the central focus of your application lifecycle is often a continuous integration server. That server fetches code from your version control system, tracks changes included in each release and the user stories associated with them, runs automated unit tests, and produces binaries for distribution.

We have extended Jenkins with mobile clients and plugins so that it can distribute software and release notes to our mobile beta users.

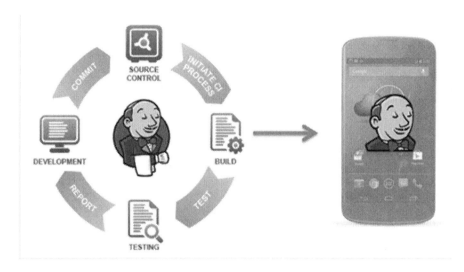

Mobile acceptance tests

There are a number of acceptance tests you can run during continuous integration builds. You can automate many of them with both commercial and open-source tools such as the Android emulator plug-in for Jenkins (see https://wiki.jenkins-ci.org/display/JENKINS/Android+Emulator+Plugin) in combination with MonkeyRunner.

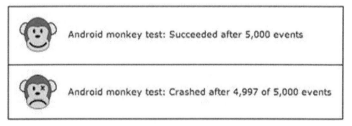

However, there are a number of usability acceptance tests that cannot be run automatically, because they require people to use the features on a device and provide real feedback with real thumbs on the touchscreen.

Allow real beta testers to put their hands on the application and use it. Whenever they find problems they can report them directly within the application. Feedback can be automatically collected and organized into acceptance test reports.

Auto-dynamic release notes

The goal of continuous delivery is to have everybody aligned to the "latest and greatest" version of the software. This avoids troubleshooting on older branches and keeps customers engaged with the latest features of the software.

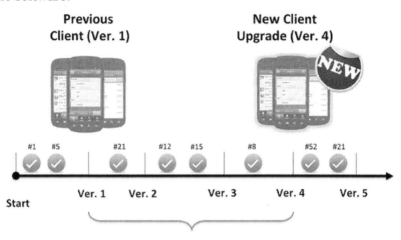

Release notes for Client upgrade

In order to avoid losing control of which features are contained in a specific software upgrade, a new way of composing release notes is needed.

1. **Always associate stories to commit changes.** Include in each source code commit the ticket-id of the feature that has been included in that change. Never mix up multiple features in a single commit, because that makes it difficult to isolate the effect of each feature in case of a failure.

2. **Auto-extract release notes at build time.** During the continuous integration build, cross-reference the changes coming from your commits with the list of tickets referenced. This builds up your release notes so they are automatically associated with the correct release artifacts.

3. **Dynamically compose notes for each client upgrade.** Each client migrating from Version X to Version Y will include a different set of features. This results from the union of all tickets resolved in the code between the two versions. Users need to see reports on the full set of changes included in their "release jump."

Conclusion

Mobile application development is moving fast. Continuous integration and deployment needs to be adapted for the mobile experience so you can include your clients in the loop, show them what you are delivering, and collect their real feedback in real time.

Tools such as JenkinsMobi can facilitate this feedback loop by integrating all the elements of your Agile Lifecycle Management (ALM) into the mobile experience, and by integrating feedback about the client software into your issue tracking backlog. The cycle looks like this:

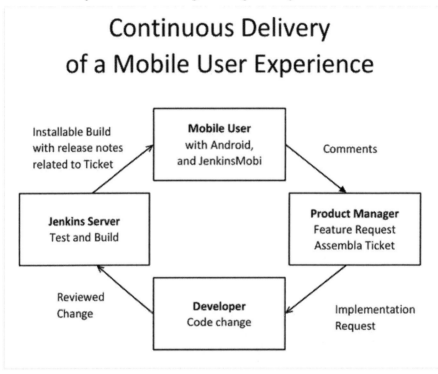

Working With Clients

Do you build software for clients, or for internal IT customers? Speed those projects up with continuous agile. Here are tactics that we use to remove barriers to starting a project, release faster, and get value and profits earlier.

 Continuous delivery is now the standard practice for small, design focused projects that produce Web sites, Web apps, and mobile apps. It's great for situations where you need to design and refine a user experience. It's also good for situations where you want to improve the product by learning from data on usage and user engagement. You can show the product, get feedback, and respond with improvements on a fast cycle. When you launch a continuous project, strengthen it by focusing on user experience design and online usage data. It is an opportunity to truly do product design, rather than just implementation.

Negotiating

Get started as soon as possible. Most development projects have a surprisingly long "fuzzy front end." If you can reduce this planning time, your customer will get value faster, and you will get paid faster.

Never do anything with a fixed scope, meaning a fixed, predefined set of deliverables or specification. You will gain two advantages

1) You will have room for improvement. A continuous project should be discovering and improving the end product during the development phase.

2) You will start earlier. It takes a long time to negotiate a fixed price, fixed scope agreement. A lot of things need to be specified and estimated. If you just get started, you might find that you finish a big chunk of work in the time that was previously required for planning.

Negotiating a budget will be challenging if the buyer wants a fixed scope for a fixed price. However, you can promise something almost as good. You can promise a fixed price and a fixed TIME. The continuous process gives you a much higher probability of delivering in a fixed time than other approaches. And, staying in the fixed time box protects your margins, because your costs are controlled by the amount of time that you spend.

You should bill for your level of effort - a specific price in each week, for a specific team size in each week. The customer can cancel after any week. You should get paid for each week of effort, and you should show your work each week.

You can promise a simple guaranteed deliverable, plus as much extra stuff as you can fit into the fixed time.

Staffing

You should accelerate your project by using all available resources. You want to engage the client with real time collaboration and response. Include your own team, anyone at the client that has useful skills and knowledge, and then grab any contractors or outsourcers that you think you can use. We call this a "blended team." I like to take over as the boss and drive this process.

Overstaff the kickoff. It's true that adding ignorant people to a software project is a hassle, and it can slow you down. However, that is only true later in the project. At the beginning of the project, everyone is ignorant. So, it doesn't slow you down to have more people. You can remove the extra people as soon as you identify the core team. However, you will have a reservoir of people that understand the project if you need them later. This is a trick that engineers don't like (because it lowers efficiency), but outsourcers understand, because it makes project delivery more reliable.

Launching

Start with builds, not designs. You want to do complete deploys or releases of all components, as early as possible. This will be faster and more efficient than a waterfall-style approach where you first do a mockup and other design work, and then build and release components sequentially.

For example, we recently worked on a SaaS delivery project that required three major technology components: 1) A new portal application to register users and create SaaS instances for them; 2) a cluster to manage the underlying single-tenant applications; 3) a proxy server to send traffic to the correct instance of the application and handlo failover.

In an old-style development project, we would first design the portal and make sure that we liked the UI. Then we would build the underlying components and attach them to the portal. In this continuous development project, we proceeded in this order:

1. Set up code repositories, development environments, and build scripts for each component. The UI mockup makes up a fourth component of this system.

2. Set up a staging server containing all of the components, with no functionality. Essentially each component is just a "hello world" build. Start automated releases.

3. Wire the pieces together to create functionality. This happens in parallel with the UI design.

This build-first approach makes projects easier to manage by sharing your work. Instead of working to an abstract plan, you move quickly to requests and responses. It also motivates the developer of each component, since they know their work will be shown. And, it prevents a buildup of problems and stress at the end of the project. You will be constantly deploying the system, and the first production release will be a well-practiced non-event.

Working Together

Let the client control the sorting of the backlog. Make them feel like they are in control of the priorities. Let them add to the backlog at any time. They will find this interaction very satisfying. As they see you respond, they may become eager to learn how to submit requests that are more clear and actionable.

Your implementation team will control the flow of items from the top of the backlog into the WIP area. Your tech lead should select items when the team is ready to work on them. Keep this power for your implementation team. You will have a happy client, and a happy team.

Set up direct communication between your implementation team members, and client team members. If you resist the urge to control communication and presentation, you will get higher efficiency and a stickier set of relationships.

Remove meetings as soon as you don't need them. At the beginning of the project you will want daily standup chats to keep your team on track, and weekly reporting to speak with the client. Reduce these meetings as soon as you can get communication and responses flowing between the teams in real time. You can remove the daily standup chat and replace it with a daily written report and an all-day chat. You can reduce the number of people on a weekly call with the client to as few as two. You reduce the need for meetings if all of the work is easy to see, release status is easy to see, and team members on both sides are communicating freely and responding promptly. Any activity or meeting that you don't do is a 100% productivity gain.

Pull work forward. If there is a question about whether to work on something today, or wait until the system is more stable, do it today. You will find and fix problems more quickly. If you are under time pressure, you should be close to feature complete after half the elapsed time of the project. You will need the other half of the time to make a quality product. Cut your deliverable to meet this rule.

Operating

Measure and monitor. You should be the expert in measuring and monitoring developer productivity, releases, usage, and user feedback. These tools will help you get the most out of your continuous development process.

Measure everything in the released software. Good monitoring will allow you to release more frequently, by giving you the confidence that you can see problems and correct them or roll them back.

Here are some charts showing the launch of the project described above. We used all of the tactics. We were running builds from week two, and we did a public release in week seven. Velocity increased steadily. The Cumulative Flow Diagram shows that we controlled the amount of work in progress, and finished each task rapidly. The stair-step pattern shows that the client had a tendency to test and close tickets on a weekly cycle. However, by the end of the project we squeezed WIP and stabilized.

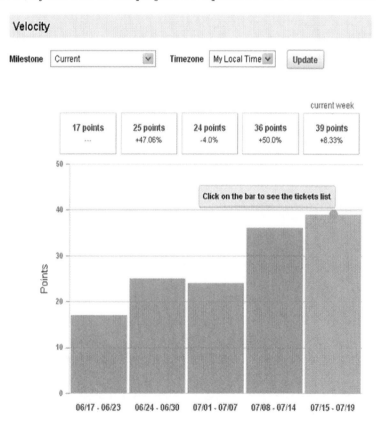

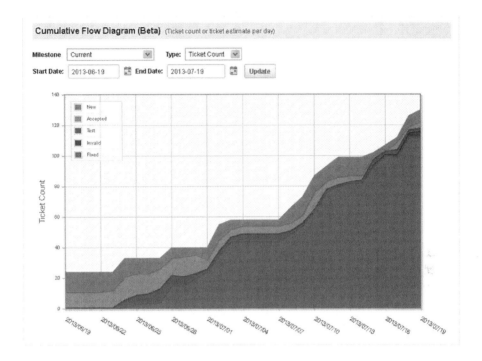

Agile Task Management

Roadmapping

Putting the best first

Agile projects start with a roadmapping and prototyping phase. In the roadmapping phase, you write down everything that you want to deliver. This is sometimes called brainstorming. You then sort those ideas in priority order. Finally, you take the top deliverables and form them into a minimum useful release.

Roadmapping delivers three things:

1. A vision and description of the completed system you want to deliver. This will explain what you are trying to accomplish, and serves as an inspiration during your incremental development.

2. A roadmap that shows the order you intend to implement the ideas.

3. A minimum useful release that you can show to your customers. This consists of the first deliverables on the top of the roadmap. This is the most important and essential output from the roadmapping process.

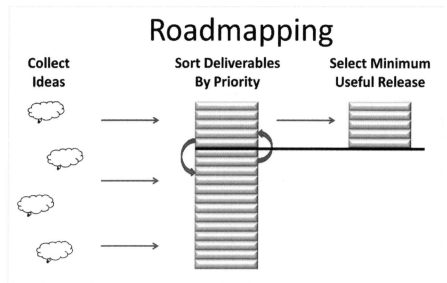

Roadmapping

| **Collect Ideas** | **Sort Deliverables By Priority** | **Select Minimum Useful Release** |

The roadmapping process:

1. Brainstorm. Collect all requests and ideas. In brainstorming, you don't filter very much. You take all of the ideas, and later you sort through them and throw out the weaklings. It's helpful to try to organize them as stories - capabilities that users actually want, described in terms of a role, a goal, and an action. Stories will come from roles - people that want them, or target users. Often your idea contributors come from these distinct roles.

2. Optional: Add information by categorizing the ideas, voting on the most important, and estimating the effort required.

3. Incrementalize. For each idea that you want to deliver, break it into a simple first version, with a series of improvements.

4. Sort by priority. Your next release should come from the items on the top of the list.

Iterations, Releases and Milestones

After completing a roadmapping process, you might want to divide your roadmap into iterations, which can be called releases or milestones. Then you can see approximately which features are assigned to each milestone.

You work on the closest or "current" milestone. When you finish the current milestone you move any unfinished tasks into the next milestone.

Release Iterations

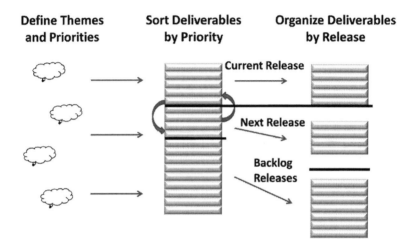

Why move to iterations? Each iteration gives you the chance to test and deliver a stable release.

Try to release on time, not when features are done. Resist pressure to expand your release. Move unfinished work to the next iteration.

Agile projects are variable scope and fixed time. You deliver some new value with every release, even if you don't always know in advance exactly what you can deliver in the allotted time. There are many benefits to this approach. You eliminate the risk that you will never deliver anything. You show your work after every iteration, so that everyone who works with you can see the status of the project. You get regular feedback on new features so you can improve them.

You can improve the plan in every iteration. Make the features better than they were in the original requirements and roadmap. This is the main benefit that you get from allowing variable scope.

You can also observe and measure velocity, the speed of delivering features.

Scrum

A scrum sprint is a formal iteration in which the team makes an accurate plan in order to increase predictability. They also work on improving productivity by measuring velocity and doing retrospectives.

Scrum is structured around three rituals: sprint planning, a daily standup meeting, and retrospectives.

Ritual 1: Sprint planning

The team starts with a single backlog, sorted by priority. When team members make an iteration plan, they pull items off the top into a "Sprint backlog" (the current iteration).

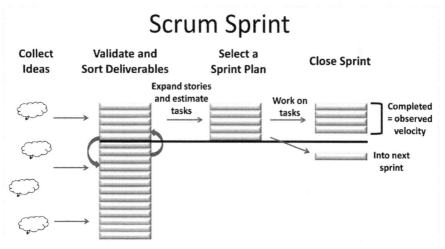

Sprint planning often involves the following steps:

- Estimating the size or difficulty of each task using "points". Points are a relative measure: tasks with a similar number of points should require similar amounts of work. Points help teams compare the amount of work in succeeding sprints.

- Measuring velocity - the number of points completed in previous sprints - to provide a guide for the number of points that can be completed in the current sprint.

- Writing backlog tasks as "stories" with functional user goals.

Stories are an improvement over just writing down tasks because they provide a better guide to actual user requirements. They also group many implementation tasks into one story, which simplifies the backlog. Sprint teams expand stories into implementation tasks when they pull them into the current sprint.

Managers like the predictability that comes from good sprint planning. Sprint planning can be a great place to get everyone involved in feature design.

However, sprint planning is also a source of problems. Velocity measurement only works when teams are stable, so teams are discouraged from growing their capacity. Planning and estimating takes time from other team activities, and they are hard to perform with large and distributed teams. If you have multiple teams you will want to have "Scrum of Scrum" meetings where team representatives can ask each other about dependencies and tasks they need completed in the current sprint.

Ritual 2: Daily Scrum or Standup meeting

Once per day the team gathers for a "Scrum"" or "Standup" meeting. The participants stand, so they will not get too comfortable, and the meeting must be short, so everyone can go back to work. Each person says:

- What I did since the last standup meeting.

- What I am working on and will do today. Pay attention to this, because often people are not working on the top priority, or they get stuck on one task. If you have a different priority, this is a chance to ask them to switch.

- Needs and obstacles. This is where other team members and "management" can jump in and help.

Daily scrum or standup meetings are a good idea for co-located teams. Distributed teams should skip them. Instead, distributed teams should run a continuous chat and post a form online that covers "what I did," "what I will do" and obstacles.

During the implementation of the Sprint, more and more tasks get completed. This can be represented as a "burn up" on our cumulative flow diagram. If everything goes well, the line will be quite straight, and most of the tasks will be complete at the end of the sprint. Remember to release on schedule!

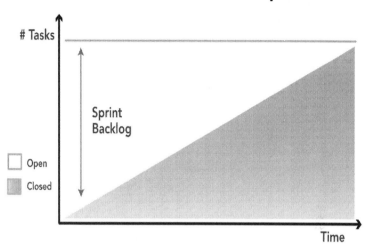

Idealized Scrum Sprint

You can map the progress of your sprint on a cardwall where you define the status columns to match your process.

Ritual 3: Retrospective

After the iteration is completed, the team does a "retrospective" to discuss what can be improved in the next sprint. It is a good idea to schedule these discussions on a regular basis, and constantly work to improve team productivity and happiness. You can also use a happiness survey.

Summary

Scrum is an extremely popular methodology because it tends to raise the level of team motivation, interaction and commitment. The end goal is a "self-managed team."

Scrum enthusiasts encourage teams to stick very closely to the "three rituals," and they disparage any deviation as "scrumbut." However, their recommendations only work well for co-located teams with 5-10 team members, and for major release cycles longer than one month.

If you don't fit that model exactly, you should make some of the adjustments recommended in the following sections of this book.

Scrumban

Planning a Scrum sprint is a difficult task, especially if you have distributed teams and can't get everyone into one meeting room. You might find that Scrum iteration planning is a waste of time altogether. However, you still need to deliver scheduled releases reliably.

In this situation you can use the Scrumban pattern. In fact, I find that many teams are using Scrumban already, without giving it a name.

In the Scrumban pattern, you skip the iteration plan. When team members are ready to work on a task, the tech leads or team members take one off the top of the project backlog. When they finish one task, they go back and get another one. This can continue for some time, until you are ready to finish your release.

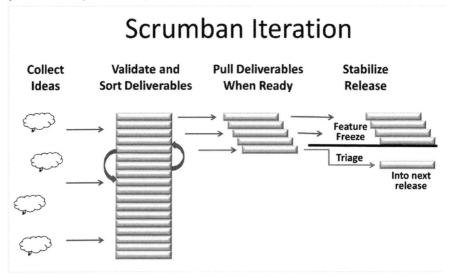

When you are getting ready to release you do a feature freeze. You stop allowing team members to take new deliverable tasks. They will work on finishing the existing tasks and closing new bug reports. You also find any tasks that are not likely to be completed by the end of the release, and move them out of the release and back to the top of the project backlog. This is a form of "triage."

Idealized Scrumban Release

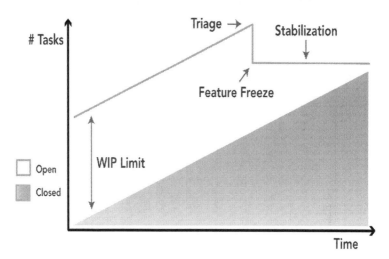

Some guidelines

I find that the feature freeze often happens about two-thirds of the way through the iteration. The exact length of the feature freeze is determined by the length of time that it takes to fully test your deliverables

You should do a retrospective after each release and figure out what you want to do better in the next release. Remember to watch the actual velocity of each release for changes in productivity.

Kanban / Continuous

Kanban eliminates the sprints or iterations of Scrum and Scrumban processes. Move to Kanban if:

- You want to release more frequently

- Customers demand changes that don't fall into a fixed release schedule

- You want to organize distributed teams without meetings

- Iterations are taking longer and longer to test and stabilize. This is a sign that you need to test and release smaller batches and move toward continuous delivery

- You are using continuous delivery to test and release code

Kanban is the simplest type of task management, but it requires the most sophisticated code management.

"Kanban" means "cardwall" in Japanese. Team members "pull" tasks to work on and put "cards" representing the tasks on a physical or online "cardwall," where everyone can see their status and progress. Team members work until the tasks are done, and only then pull new ones. This is a continuous flow process without any stopping points for big releases.

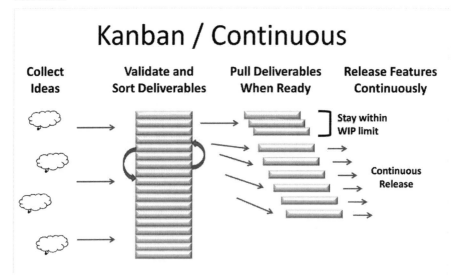

Kanban / Continuous

| Collect Ideas | Validate and Sort Deliverables | Pull Deliverables When Ready | Release Features Continuously |

Stay within WIP limit

Continuous Release

When you design a Kanban process, you set up a cardwall with status columns. Each column represents a step in your task lifecycle or workflow. For example, a cardwall might have columns for "New," "Design," "Program," "Test," "Deploy" and "Done."

WIP (Work in Progress)

There are always tasks on the cardwall, which are called "Work In Progress" or WIP. You want to make sure that, if a task is on the cardwall, someone is working on it. Therefore WIP is always limited, typically to one or two tasks per team member.

Limiting WIP is THE KEY TOOL that Kanban and Lean use to bring order out of chaos.

Kaizen, retrospective or happiness survey

You will journey with Kaizen - continuous improvement. Do retrospectives and other analysis to find ways to improve. There is no specific time after a release to hold a retrospective and discuss process improvements. Or, you can cover all of your team´s improvement ideas in one place with a "Happiness Survey." Every one, two or four weeks ask your team "what feels best," "what feels worst," and "what would increase your happiness?" The responses will yield a lot of actionable advice.

Keep the process flowing by looking for:

- **Bottlenecks.** These are cardwall status columns where tasks are piling up. For example, you may see a lot of tasks that are piled up in the testing column. In Kanban terms, this is exceeding the Work In Progress limit for that column. When you see this, move your effort from the step before the pileup downstream to the step where the pileup occurred. For example, If you have too many tasks in the test column, you ask programmers to stop adding more and move downstream to finish the tests. I call this "unblocking from the end."

- **Stuck tasks (or "stuck tickets" in Assembla terms)** - These are tasks that have not moved forward recently. If a task has not moved to the next step in several days it is dying inventory, and it shows that you have a problem to fix.

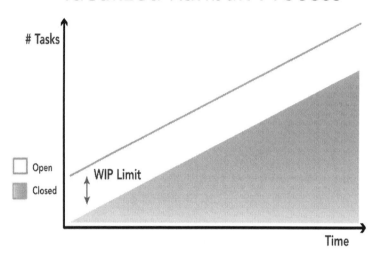

Idealized Kanban Process

Kanban for any business process

Kanban is a general-purpose technique for organizing work. You can take almost any business process and show it on a Kanban board. The basic formula is to find "sources of demand" (the people that give you tasks). They put cards on the board in a backlog area. Then you map the process to show the stages that each task goes through.

This has a number of benefits. Your work is visible, so you spend less time explaining what you are working on. Each "source of demand" can see where their task fits in the queue. You can work with less stress by limiting "work in progress." You can deliver high priority tasks faster. You can improve the work by measuring cycle time and seeing bottlenecks.

You can make individual Kanban boards to show the workload of individuals. This is useful for "shared resources," such as designers working on multiple projects where it is important to know if they are overloaded or if they have available capacity.

You can use Kanban for almost any time scale. A system operations team could use it to track things that need to be done today. A marketer could use it for campaigns that take a month to execute. A strategic planning group could use it for a 3-month planning and budgeting process.

In contrast, Scrum is only appropriate for specialized situations. It's a team methodology that works if you have teams of 5 to 10 people. It is a batch process that only works if you can wait one to eight weeks for a deliverable, and if you finish deliverables in one to eight weeks. Scrum fits programming teams, but not operations, marketing, planning or other non-development functions. Only use Scrum if your team is 5-10 people and your delivery time is between one and eight weeks. Otherwise, use Kanban.

Lean Theory

You can improve your results by using lean manufacturing ideas pioneered in the automobile industry. These methods have proven successful in eliminating waste and costs, improving manufacturing quality, and allowing companies to bring to market complex new products (such as new automobile models) in half the time or less compared to older techniques.

Principle of pull

A lean process is organized by "the Principle of Pull." A worker or team pulls a task when there is capacity to finish it. This saves management time, since there is no complex process to assign tasks. However, it is often necessary to remind eager team members that they should only pull one or two tasks at a time.

The Principle of Pull also applies to building releases. Changes are pulled into releases when they are ready. This reduces stress and improves quality, because there is less pressure to rush features into production to meet a fixed release schedule. It also makes it easier to enforce coding standards and test coverage, since you can refuse to pull code that doesn´t meet those standards.

Reduce inventory and work in progress

"Lean" manufacturing methods focus on reducing the inventory of physical parts that are waiting to be assembled into a finished product. "Lean" software methodologies focus on reducing work in progress, which are the tasks that have been started but not completed. Reducing WIP has a number of advantages:

- Each task gets finished faster, since the team is working on fewer tasks. Tasks are more likely to be completely finished, since each task must be completely finished before starting a new task. If you find that you are waiting a long time for stories to be finished and released, you need to reduce your work in progress.

- Less time and money tied up in features that are not released and not producing value.

- Less chance of software becoming obsolete or outdated before delivery

- Greater visibility into problems in the process. Any place where active tasks are waiting becomes obvious.

Measurement

Measure so that you can improve! Kanban enthusiasts typically focus on metrics related to speed. Speed is good.

Lead time - The time that it takes to move a task from first pull to finished. You can look at averages, and also at slow tasks that stick at the 90th percentile. You can see these on your cumulative flow diagram. You want lead time to be as short as possible. If it starts to lengthen, reduce your work in progress.

You might find that delivery is quite fast after you pull tasks, but some tasks spend a lot of time waiting in the backlog or being "groomed" with appropriate information. This is because there are really two kinds of lead time. Delivery lead time is the interval between starting work on a task and completing it. End-to-end lead time is the interval between accepting a task into the backlog or queue and completing it. If your users or customers perceive your responsiveness as related to end-to-end lead time, then you need to monitor that form of lead time and address the factors causing it to lengthen.

High priority lead time - It feels great and relieves a lot of stress if you can deliver high priority items quickly.

Cycle time - You can measure the amount of time that tasks spend in a specific status column. This is the cycle time for that column. Typically, most stages are fast, and a few of them are slow. That's gives you specific opportunities for improvement. If you find that a stage is slow, you will want to set a "WIP limit" for that stage - a maximum number of tasks that can pile up there. That motivates you to fix the problem.

Throughput or Velocity- How much can you do in a month? You can take simple averages, or you can do increasingly complex Monte Carlo simulations to give you an idea for how much you can do next month.

Quality - In software development, a typical indicator of a quality problem is a ticket that goes backwards in status. For example, tickets can go backwards from "Test" to "In Progress" if they fail a test. You want to measure the frequency of these events and see if you can reduce them.

One-piece flow

In manufacturing, workers are more productive if, once they start on a piece they can finish it without waiting for additional parts to arrive or being pulled off to work on other pieces. In software terms, developers will be more productive if they can finish one story without waiting for a lot of other stories to be completed or being asked to switch between several tasks.

This simple principle turns out to have a variety of implications:

- Tasks get finished faster. This speeds up the completion of high priority changes and the delivery of value to customers.

- Processes are more predictable. Delivery times are based on the work required for each task, not on the number and priority of tasks assigned to each developer. This makes scheduling easier and reduces management work. You many even be able to eliminate status reporting on stories, because you know that once started they will come out quickly.

- Bottlenecks are visible. For example, if tasks are piling up in "test" status, you can see it on your Kanban cardwall and take action by moving developers from programming to testing. This gets stuck features released faster and rebalances your capacity at the same time. A continuous flow processes is only as fast as its slowest point, so removing bottlenecks optimizes processes and increases overall output and productivity.

- Developers are more productive because they have less "switching" time. Switching among tasks and bug fixes requires both physical setup time to prepare test environments and mental setup time to remember details and issues. Developers who focus on one task at a time are much more productive and make fewer mistakes.

- Deliverables take as long as they need, rather than being shoehorned into fixed release cycles. A high priority bug fix should go through in a few hours. A big new feature or a major refactoring might take weeks. Allowing the right amount of time for each task reduces stress on developers and leads to more realistic schedules.

- One-piece flow allows the process to be non-blocking. If one developer is stuck and can´t release, the other developers can continue to pull and release work. This is a major reason why continuous processes are much more scalable than batch iterations.

Match Kanban with Continuous Delivery

In a software Kanban process you want to test, finish and release each change. You can´t easily finish a task if you use a naïve testing process where you put your changes into a release candidate and wait for some sort of batch testing. Later in this guide we will cover techniques for Continuous Delivery that allow you to immediately test and release each change.

Code Management

Contributors

You can skip this chapter

You can skip this chapter if you aren't interested in learning more about the details of code repositories and code versioning workflows.

Contributors

I will use the word "contributor" to refer to programmers who contribute changes to code, and to everyone else who makes useful changes. It is a better term than "resource," because it focuses attention on what we want (contributions), rather than implying that there are objects to be controlled (resources).

Software is an ecosystem, and some contributors are likely to come from outside of your existing team and management structure.

Code contribution workflows

In the old days, there was just one version of a piece of software and several programmers could edit it, like a bunch of painters working on different areas of a fresco.

With the Internet and modern version control systems, we have a lot more choices in the workflows we use to collect and handle changes to code. We might test each change personally before adding it to the shared version. This is a "maintainer" workflow. Before merging changes to the shared version, we might ask some team members to vote on it. This is a team review workflow. We might have a machine test the changes and warn the contributor if there is a problem. Choosing the right code contribution workflow for your environment will help you scale up software development to bigger teams and faster releases.

Version Control Basics

A development project with more than one contributor requires a source code repository (repo) or "version control system" (VCS). These systems allow two or more programmers to work on the same set of files. Every programmer can "commit" changes to files. Other participants can then get the changes.

There are a few differences between a programmer's VCS and a normal file sharing system. A VCS keeps track of the file system as it existed before each change. If you decide later that there is a problem with a change, you can "roll back" to a previous version. This safety valve, also used in wikis, gives you the security to make changes. A VCS also shows you details about each change, down to the line that was changed, so you can track down problems.

A VCS also helps merge changes from different contributors. If Bill and Ted each edit different files, then Bill can get Ted's changed file, and Ted can get Bill's changed file. If they both edit the same file, then there is a conflict. The early VCS systems (and their modern descendants like Dropbox and Google Drive) give you both copies (like file_Ted and file_Bill) and let you pick the one that you want. A modern programmer's VCS will merge the changes. If Bill and Ted edited different lines in a text file, the merge can automatically include both sets of changes. If Bill and Ted edit the same line, and the VCS can't figure out what to do, it will ask the recipient to pick the version of the line that he or she wants.

Different VCS systems have different strategies for merging changes in moved and edited files.

Centralized VCS

A centralized VCS is a server, like a file server. Contributors use client software to pull out a chunk of the files into a local "working copy" or "workspace." They can send changes (commits) to the server, and get updates back with changes from other developers.

A centralized VCS can handle large files and very large repositories. Not every file needs to be replicated to clients, which is important for designers, and for building games that have big graphical files.

Subversion (SVN) is the most popular centralized VCS. Subversion operations are simple and easily learned by everyone on your team. However, Subversion in its current version has a very limited merge operation, which means that it is difficult to use it for merge-intensive workflows like feature and task branches, branch review, and cascading promotion.

Subversion works well for three workflows:

- An informal workflow where people share and synchronize design assets.

- An iterative process with release branches.

- A centralized continuous delivery process, where all developers contribute to one "active trunk."

Subversion will easily synchronize developers for centralized continuous integration (CI) and centralized continuous delivery (CD). Historically, centralized CI and CD have evolved with Subversion.

Distributed VCS

In a distributed version control system, or DVCS, every user has a complete copy of the repository on his or her machine. Users move code changes around with peer-to-peer operations like "push" and "pull." However, in practice few teams use peer-to-peer exclusively; almost all teams use a centralized portal to share code and changes.

Distributed VCS systems need to be good at merging, because they merge every time code moves from one person or place to another. They are good at moving code around the cloud. They have produced a burst of innovation in coding workflows that involve contributing, moving, testing and merging changes.

There are several good open source distributed VCS systems. The most popular system is Git, originally designed by Linus Torvalds to handle code contributions for Linux. Git is loved by programmers because it provides a powerful way for them to manage their local code. However, it is implemented with more than 40 commands, so non-programmers find it confusing.

DVCS systems have created a revolution in the scale of open source software development. Anyone on the Internet can become a contributor to a project by making a copy or "clone" of the project repository and working on it. In contrast, a centralized system limits the number of contributors by requiring an administrator to grant permission to use the centralized repository.

DVCS systems have spawned new workflows that are very useful for continuous delivery. A DVCS system needs to be good at moving and merging "changesets." These bundles of code changes can be routed on any path you want, including release branches, task branches, feature clones, branch review and cascading integration. You can use Git to implement any of the workflows in this guide.

Streams

Centralized repository systems like ClearCase, AccuRev and Perforce can use a topology called "streams." Streams give you a structured form of branching, forking and merging, where you can feed changes down predefined paths between individuals, teams and integrated builds. It naturally supports the cascading process. You can use a stream topology to implement any of the workflows we will discuss.

Perforce

Perforce is a centralized repository that has some of the advantages of Subversion. It can handle big files and big repositories, and is often used to build games with spectacular graphics. Compared with Subversion, it has a good structure for merging and tracking changesets. That allows it to implement many of the merge-based workflows that are coming out of the DVCS world. It can even host a centralized view of Git repositories.

As a centralized repository, Perforce requires some administration and places more restrictions on contributors than a DVCS. However, it has an advantage over a DVCS if you are assembling multiple systems from multiple components. In Perforce, you can assemble systems just by making mix-and-match views of the shared components. With a DVCS you would be required to copy and maintain multiple copies of the components.

Prototyping

Prototyping does not require any pattern or workflow. One or two programmers contribute changes to a single version and show the results whenever they feel like it.

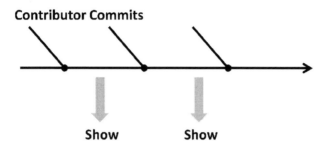

The goal of prototyping is to figure out as quickly and cheaply as possible whether a technical approach will work, or a new product or function will be useful and interesting. Prototyping provides a spark of innovation to light up a structured process. You need prototyping to try out new things, so it is a very important skill to maintain in any development organization.

Prototyping teams should be small – one or two people. Small teams work faster and more productively. They are also cheaper. You will lower your cost of innovation if you know when to drop into prototyping mode to try something new.

You should ask the best person available to prototype. That person will have the widest range of skills and will require the least help from others. Using the best person makes the effort smaller and faster.

Don't try to "help" with project management. Prototyping will move faster if it is an individual exploration.

You should manage by timeboxing. Prototypers should have a time limit, show their work on demand, and present it to peers.

Don't be afraid to ask two people to do prototypes of the same thing. Engineers hate to think they are wasting effort, but this type of redundancy is a cheap way to bring out innovative ideas.

Shift to a more structured methodology as soon as three or more people are involved.

Iterative Releases

Before releasing your prototype to users, you will want to make sure that it is fully tested. You can do this by moving to an iterative release pattern.

With iterative releases, you test your system, and when you have a stable version you make a "release branch" in your repo that contains the source code. This allows you to test, fix and distribute the stable release branch, while experimenting with and enhancing a separate development version.

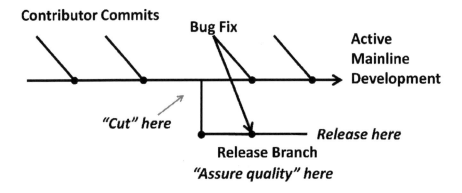

You might find a bug in your release. In that case, you will need to commit the bug fix both to the release branch and to the development version for future releases. This is a small annoyance of the release branch system. It provides an incentive to "cut the release branch" fairly late in the process of developing a release candidate, after most bugs have been found. The later you "cut," the fewer fixes have to be applied in two places, and the closer you get to continuous delivery.

Testing release candidates

Almost all iterative release processes test a single release candidate that is built from a recent version of the "active" or "mainline" branch.

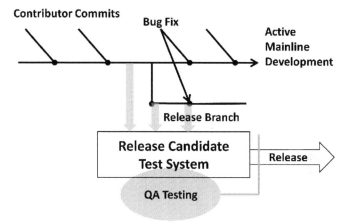

The release candidate allows you to spread out the work of testing the software. You can have a QA person test it, or you can show it to "beta test" users and get their feedback. If your project is large enough to have a QA team, you will be tempted to give the QA team final responsibility for deciding when a release candidate is ready to release.

Getting releases out

To be considered "Agile," you have to deliver releases on time. What do you do if you have promised a release every four weeks, but your release candidate is not stable? I am often asked this question by development teams that are stuck in a cycle of never releasing. They always have good reasons why they aren't ready to release. Don't get stuck this way. Your bosses or investors will get frustrated and put you under unpleasant amounts of pressure.

You can break the roadblock by telling the team that they WILL release, but they can decide the recipients. Instead of releasing to everyone, you can release just to your internal team, to close friends and partner companies, or to selected friendly customers.

Moving from informal to iterative

When you move from informal development to iterative, tested releases, you will need to make infrastructure decisions regarding:

1) **Task management**. How will you keep track of feature requests, bug reports and tasks?

2) **Code management**. Where will you put your code, and what type of code contribution workflow will programmers use?

3) **Build, test, and deploy scripts and infrastructure**. How will you build the release candidate and the distributed or deployed version, and make the process repeatable?

Review Flows

You can implement a workflow to review and test each change submitted to your active, mainline version. This requires some extra work from your developers. However, it solves some specific problems and makes your development process more scalable because:

- You can motivate developers and QA staff to create and run the automated tests that make a continuous integration process work. You do this by refusing to review and accept any code change until after it has been tested. Code review works better than any other method to enforce testing standards.

- You can include new contributors, virtual team members, partner companies and other distributed contributors. Instead of looking over people's shoulders in the office, you use the review process to vet work from contributors across the globe.

- Your mainline build is more stable. You spend less time waiting for fixes. You can support team members in many time zones, and you can release more frequently and with less batch testing.

There are a lot of variations on review workflows. I will discuss them here so that you can see why we recommend either a review workflow based on temporary branches (for mainline development), or a branch and merge workflow.

Post-commit reviews

In an old-style review process, team members would gather to critique code after it was committed to the mainline. This is a good way to discuss and enforce coding standards and solve architecture problems. However, it reduces the stability of the mainline and requires extra work, and the recommendations for future changes are easy to ignore. I have seen a lot of teams try this type of review and abandon it. Don't make your team do these "post-commit" reviews. They are annoying.

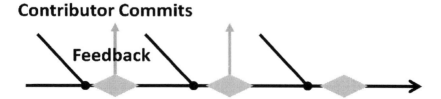

Contributor Commits

Feedback

Pre-commit reviews with patch files

Instead of committing a change directly, a developer can make a patch file containing his or her change and post it to a patch-based review system like ReviewBoard, Mondrian or Crucible. Other developers can then apply the patch, comment on it, and accept or reject it. An even older technique used by some Apache projects is to attach the patch to an email and send it to an email list for review.

This "pre-commit" review is more effective than post-commit review. It can be combined with "preflight" automated tests that run locally. Google has used these tactics very successfully. However, it is annoying to go through several steps to make a patch, post a patch, test a patch, and fix a new patch.

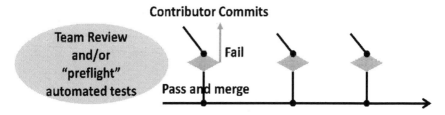

Temporary review branches

Instead of making patches, you can put changes into a temporary branch in the VCS. This is the system used by a Gerrit "change" (called a "task branch" in other systems). It is easier to fix and update a branch than to reconstruct a patch. When the branch passes review, the system can merge it automatically to the mainline.

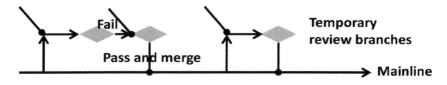

The folks at Google used to run a mainline continuous process with a bulletin board for reviewing patches. When they adopted Git for Android development they decided to upgrade from patches to review branches. They built a Web-based code contribution system called Gerrit which turns Git commits into "changes" that go into temporary branches. Users can comment on the changes and vote on them. Changes get merged when they receive a minimum number of votes.

Google uses Gerrit to accept contributions from thousands of people working on various parts of Android, and it has become popular for other development projects. Assembla implements a streamlined version of this workflow with protected branches.

The review or task branch gives you a clever place to put automated testing so that code is always tested before it is delivered to reviewers.

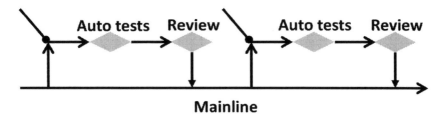

Perforce uses a feature called a "shelf" to save changes in a temporary branch for review.

Why use review or task branches?

I believe that the system of putting changes into branches for test and review completely obsoletes the older "pre-commit" and patch-based review systems because:

- **It is much easier to apply automated testing to real branches.**

- There are fewer steps for developers who want to test, review and comment, and they never need to leave their normal code browser.

- If reviewers want to fix something in the contribution, they just make a change in the review branch.

Reviewing changes in temporary branches is a good next step for any team that is contributing to a centralized trunk or master. The key concept here is that we are using "temporary" review branches. Contributors are working on a shared version, with short-lived branches for review. The advantages of this approach include:

- A simple transition from a workflow of contributing directly to the mainline. Changes are small for contributors, and for configuring build and test systems.

- It is easy for contributors to maintain. They always start working with a copy of the mainline. If you have a centralized team of DevOps and tech leads, they can provide more control and support.

- It is scalable. Multiple people can vote on changes to the same system and merging is automated.

Review branches are the tool of choice for teams that are upgrading from a mainline or trunk-based process, and for teams that have full-time reviewers (tech leads or maintainers).

The review branch process can scale to large numbers of contributors - for example, in Android and Eclipse development. However, contributors cannot work without timely review from the tech lead team, so if you use temporary review or task branches you should have a full-time reviewing team.

You can implement review branches with:

- Gerrit and Git, or Assembla Git protected branches. These tools create review branches automatically.

- Perforce changelists. The changelist is an excellent review branch container. You can get the review workflow in Assembla or in the Perforce Swarm product.

- Git merge requests and pull requests, if you set up testing for these requests.

There is a review branch workflow for Subversion which we will extend to support centralized continuous delivery, but it needs some refinement.

Cascading Integration

In a cascading pattern, the contributor (an individual or team) sends changes to a downstream version which is more stable and tested with other components. Cascading produces a more integrated and stable release version.

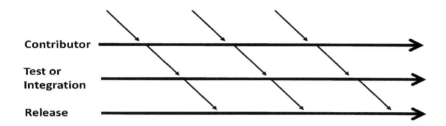

The cascading pattern is useful when:

- You have a lot of components to integrate. For example, in the Linux development process, changes move from component maintainers to "lieutenants," who test the integration of subsystems, to a "benevolent dictator" (sometimes Linus Torvalds himself), who assembles a complete kernel release.

- You have strict requirements for testing, security, or compliance. You can address your requirements at the more stable downstream levels. You protect your developers from the hassle of these requirements, so they can run a more productive and continuous process

The picture above shows three levels: 1) the contributor version; 2) a test or integration version, which would typically be used to test work from several contributing people or teams; 3) the stable release version.

You could add a fourth level to integrate more components, to do user acceptance testing, or to perform localization. However, there is a limit to the number of levels that you can use, because the cascading pattern introduces delays into the bug fix process. These delays also make the cascading pattern poorly suited for continuous delivery, although it works if you use CI and CD at the contributor level.

In the diagram below, a bug (bug 1) was found in the production release. We need to make a bug fix for all versions, not just the production version. The contributor updates his version from the production version to reproduce and fix the bug. This is the correct and normal way to unify developers in a cascading process. However, the bug fix must be applied at several levels to make it back to the production version. The process for fixing Bug 2 is more efficient, because it is closer to the developer. However, we now have a situation where at least one contributor is working on an intermediate version, rather than staying connected to the shared stable version.

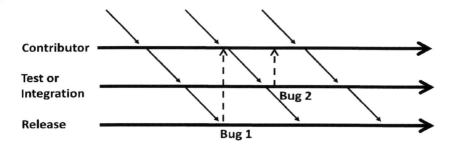

Because the path for fixes is complicated, cascading workflows are going out of style and being replaced by workflows with shorter fix paths.

Branching and Forking

In branch and merge patterns, each contributor maintains his own version of the software (a branch or a fork). The contributor copies the mainline at the beginning, then maintains it by merging changes from the mainline to stay up to date. When the contributor has a complete change to contribute, he can merge it directly to the mainline, or put a "merge request" or "pull request" into a review system.

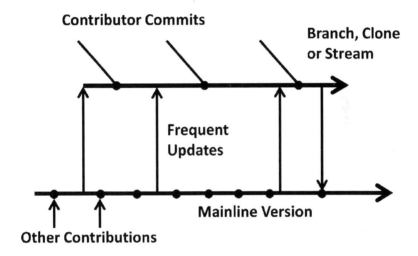

This is a very flexible pattern that can implement several of the previous patterns.

Informal. You can update frequently and merge each change directly, without review

Branch review. You will naturally get the branch review pattern if you make "task branches" for each change that you want to work on.

Cascading. You will get a cascading pattern if you make branches or forks for each major feature or team. This is commonly called a "feature branch" pattern if you use it for features. If you use it for teams or individual contributors, you get a "maintainer" pattern where each contributor submits changes up to a maintainer, who integrates them into a bigger system.

Distributed Continuous Delivery: In the continuous delivery chapter, we will see how branches can be used to test and release each change.

Branching has several flavors, illustrated below.

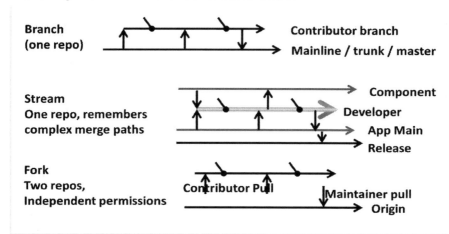

Branch: Contributors can make a branch inside any repository. Branches and branch permissions are authorized by a repository owner. This workflow makes content and changes visible to everyone in a small team.

Stream: In a stream-based system like Perforce, the developer branches remember the upstream branches that should be the source of their updates, and the downstream branches to which their changes should flow. Stream systems are useful if you are assembling a system or a developer environment from a complicated set of components. In this example, we see a branch or a workspace that has components from several other branches.

Fork: The contributor uses a DVCS (distributed version control system) like Git to make a copy of the mainline version, called a fork. When you fork, there are two copies of the code in separate repositories, with separate permissions. The owner of the fork decides when to update the fork, and the owner of the origin decides when to accept contributions. You can grant read permission to a lot of contributors, and you do not need to administer write permissions.

This is a great way to expand the number of contributors to an open source project. It is also popular for commercial development because of the flexibility that it gives to the contributor.

Update branches or forks frequently

Critics often observe that developers tend to work a long time on branches, then cause integration problems by merging big batches of code. Finding problems in these big batches of code is difficult. Branching processes will break down when contributions from the feature branches or forks are big, or difficult to merge, or contain bugs that must be resolved at the time of the merge.

This dreaded "long running branches" problem is the major reason why advocates of centralized continuous integration are opposed to distributed forking and branching.

However, you can easily avoid this problem if you update your feature branch frequently with changes from the origin. If you use branches or forks, you should:

- Merge frequently from the origin or production version to your development version. By doing frequent update, integration, and test in your development version, you can stay close to the production version.

- Test on your branch BEFORE you submit changes to the origin. You must make sure that the changes in the feature branch or fork work correctly before you submit them to be merged.

- Release changes as frequently as possible. When you release smaller amounts of code, you will find problems faster because you have fewer places to look for problems.

Merging with Git

Git uses branches and forks by default. Git has excellent support for the process of updating a branch or fork from the origin. Git has a unique feature called "rebase" which allows a contributor to update from the origin, and then deliver a changeset that is easy to merge. Rebase takes away the whole history of code exchanges leading up to the delivery of the changeset and puts all of the changes into one package.

This is a radical approach because it "rewrites history" by taking away the record of previous commits. Other VCS are designed to prevent any loss of history. It is possible that this radical approach to rebase is the reason that Git has become the most popular DVCS. As we shall see, it is important in the distributed continuous integration pattern.

Merging with Subversion

Subversion does not work well when you try to merge multiple times from the origin or trunk branch. Because of this, most Subversion users learn to avoid long-running branches, and most Subversion teams use a centralized continuous delivery model that avoids branching.

If you encounter a long-running branch in Subversion, you can use two tricks to merge it. The first is the new merge implementation in Subversion 1.8, from Julian Foad. He has updated Subversion merge so that it is smarter about moving changes between trunk and branches. As I write this in May 2013, the Apache Subversion team is testing these changes for release.

The second technique is a manual rebase. To do a manual rebase, first make a second branch from the trunk or origin, then merge your changes into the second branch and test it. This has the effect of putting all of your changes into one revision or set of revisions at the head of the branch history - the same effect as a Git rebase. After that you will find the revisions easy to merge to the trunk or origin.

Why use long-running feature branches?

We talked earlier about using temporary branches or task branches for code review. You can also use long-running feature branches or forks to do code review, with automated testing, commenting and voting. In this system, contributors to not make a temporary branch for each change. Instead, they maintain a longer running version, and they post "pull requests" or "merge requests" to tell reviewers to review and accept changes.

Long-running feature branches or forks will be useful if you:

- Assemble components into a complete system using the cascading pattern

- Have independent contributors that like to experiment, or are not part of the team with inside permissions

- Do not have full-time reviewers

Automated Testing

Goals of Automated Testing

It is a pain in the ass to build, maintain, and run automated tests. So, why do we do it?

1. Automated tests help you **release faster** by reducing the amount of manual testing needed for each release. That is why automated tests and continuous integration are essential if you release more than once every two weeks. You may find that release cycles are getting longer because it takes more and more time to test increasingly complex systems. This is a signal that you need automated testing.

2. By providing immediate feedback, automated tests **give programmers the confidence to make changes**. If your developers spend their time fixing a lot of small things, but don't have the confidence to make significant changes, you need automated testing.

However, while automated tests will tell you if you broke something that used to work, they are not very good at finding bugs in new features. Bugs usually come from a lack of understanding or perspective that will also be present in the tests. For example, I once worked with an organization that is a well-known proponent of test driven development. They wrote tests for every bit of new code, and ran them in the a local development environment. But this code was just as likely to show bugs in new features as code written without tests. In one case, the software only worked with a particular Web browser used in the local test environment (Safari), and it didn't work for actual users. After this was fixed, the tests became more useful, because they verified that the feature would continue to work.

An automated test is a script that looks for errors. It runs some of your code, and tells you whether it works as expected, or throws an error. We call it "continuous integration" when we set up servers to run automated tests frequently.

Building and maintaining automated tests is a lot of work. To get a good return on investment, use these measures of efficiency to evaluate your testing:

- **Find real problems**: The automated testing program should find enough real problems to be worth the effort. You can measure this. Your testing is working if you are giving programmers the confidence to make changes and reducing your time to test a release.

- **Avoid false alarms**: Many times a test will show a failure because of an intended change, and you will have to go back and modify the test. That's a waste of energy. Later in this chapter we will show you how to select types of tests that minimize this waste.

You don't want to look stupid in front of your engineers or give them extra work. Invest wisely by understanding why you are building tests, finding real problems, and avoiding false alarms.

Types of Tests

Automated tests should tell you when you broke something, while not generating false alarms and taking excessive time to adjust for intended changes.

Layering test types

You will typically be running more than one set of tests. Usually you start by monitoring your production release, or at least collecting bug reports. That's a type of test. You may add manual or automated regression testing to that so that you find problems before customers find them. Then you will add unit tests, so that anyone working on code can check it. In practice, you will add layers going backward from the production release in order to find errors closer and closer to the time when the code changed. This gives more confidence to developers. You should add test layers until you get to the quality level that you want.

While testing may seem like a big investment, you can optimize it by working these layers and finding the most efficient places to add tests. Keeping this in mind, let's evaluate some types of automated tests for their efficiency.

Input – output test

You can use an input-output test if the main function of your software is to transform input data into output data. You can configure a new test just by providing a new input/output pair. The test will check to see if the software output matches the sample output for each pair. This is the most efficient type of test, because it doesn't get any harder to maintain as you add more code.

Web Services form the foundation of today's scalable cloud systems. You can test Web services with a type of input-output test that calls the service and checks for expected return values.

UI regression test

A UI regression test uses a tool which simulates a user and analyzes the screens to make sure they match the previous output. For example, Selenium will write input to a Web application and check the screens that come back.

In systems where the UI is important, UI regression tests are not efficient. UIs tend to change frequently, so you spend a lot of time fixing the tests. You may need to use this type of test when your programming framework doesn't support other types of tests, or if you have a lot of old and static features to regression test. It has the advantage that it can have a graphical UI and be maintained by QA people who are not part of the core programming team.

A full regression test runs through all of the application functionality to make sure that you did not break something that seems unrelated to your changes. Full regression tests are not very efficient, and they take a long time to run. If you want to release frequently or continuously, you should not require a full regression test. If you think you need a full regression tests to prevent unexpected bugs, you should add more test layers until you do not need the full regression test.

Unit test

A unit test is a script that exercises a specific code object by initializing it, calling methods or functions, and checking the return values. Programmers write and run these tests locally as part of a test driven development process.

This is an efficient type of testing, and it is probably the most frequently used. A unit test must be built by programmers. A good programming framework will contain a structure for unit tests. If you have a good framework, it will be easy for a programmer to build a unit test, and often programmers build unit tests as part of a "test driven development" process. If you make changes to an object, it is fairly easy to find the related tests.

Most teams that use continuous integration ask the person who develops a feature or fixes a bug to also make related unit tests. They often use code review to check that these tests have been created and run.

Integration test

An integration test is a code level script (i.e., one that doesn't run the normal UI) that tests a complete process involving multiple objects. For instance, you might make a test for "submit an order" which checks to see if the inventory database is updated, if the invoice is correct, and if the person placing the order gets the right confirmation email.

An integration test requires more work to build because you have to set up more data, and you might need a mockup database. However, there are frameworks like Cucumber that walk you through the process. Integration tests have a medium level of efficiency, and you should build them for important actions if your programming framework supports them.

Service integration tests are important for managing large projects. Service integration tests run the complete app, including calls to multiple Web services. They ofen run on a centralized test system that has its own substantial database.

Code analysis

Code analysis tools like Sonar or Coverity will read your code and tell you if you structured your code in a way that is likely to cause bugs or security problems. This is not really a test because it doesn't find bugs. However, it is a useful layer of quality improvement. Code analysis is a very efficient type of test because it is totally automated. Your developers will respond well to a message that says "Good job friend. You increased your quality score from 2.9 to 3.6," even though it comes from a mindless script. You should fit in a code analysis layer if you can. In the future, these static code analysis tools will be enhanced to actively propose bug fixes and make other improvements.

Production logging and monitoring

All software should have an automated system for logging errors and reporting them automatically. You should also be collecting post-release user activity and system performance. You should be collecting user feedback and responding to it.

As you improve these capabilities and improve your reaction time, you will have a built-in system for eliminating defects and improving usability, performance and profitability. No matter what your pre-release testing plan, you should be trying to gather as much data as possible about the post-release performance of your software, and you should be trying to reduce the time that it takes your team to respond to this data.

This can be a very efficient type of testing. If your users can tolerate some errors, you can use it as a substitute for other tests. If your system is online, you can deploy to production before you merge to the mainline. Then, you watch the production system to make sure it works correctly. If there is a problem, you roll back to the mainline version. If it works correctly, you merge to mainline. This technique gives you a cleaner mainline that has code which has already been tested in production. It makes rollbacks simpler, and it gives the other developers a more stable mainline.

Test Frameworks

The first step in setting up automated testing is setting up a testing framework.

Unit test framework for your development platform

Modern development frameworks usually include a structure for automated unit tests. This gives programmers a place to put test scripts, a way to set up test data, and a way to run the scripts locally. Look for a test framework that matches your development platform and includes both unit tests and integration tests. If you do not have a test framework, then you may need to rely on input/output tests and UI regression tests.

Continuous Integration server

You can run a continuous integration process by asking developers to run tests on a development version of the code on their own workstations. However, this can take a long time. You want to improve your return on investment and your social structure by making testing fast and easy for developers.

A shared test system will run faster, share build results with everyone, and show problems to the team. That is why many teams use a Continuous Integration server – software that is specifically designed to build software and run tests. Popular CI servers include Jenkins, Cruise Control, and Tinderbox. With the miracle of cloud computing, you can allocate new test servers as needed. Cloud providers are even extending this idea to mobile apps, which aren't usually built on servers.

Production logging and monitoring

If you are considering continuous delivery, you should make serious efforts to log and monitor your running software. Actual user experience is the ultimate test of your software, and your ability to see user problems and respond to them quickly will give you the confidence to do everything else.

If you run an online system, you should have dashboards that show you load, performance, error rates and feature usage in real time. You should be able to compare the times before and after a release. If you distribute your software, you should add an option for the software to phone home with error messages and with statistics about load, performance and feature usage. You should log and report error messages. You are not doing a good job if users are manually reporting error messages. Stack errors should be automatically posted back to you and turned into bug fix tickets.

Social Framework

The Social Framework is the most important part of your automated testing initiative. If you want your developers to build and maintain tests, you will need a social structure that encourages them to do it.

The people that approve releases also make the tests

Your social framework will be a lot stronger if the people who approve and start releases are also the people who make the automated tests. Nobody wants the pain of approving a release, and then rushing back from Friday night beers when it breaks something.

In most continuous release shops the developers approve releases, and the QA team is available to help them on a consulting basis. In these organizations, developers make useful test scripts.

Code review

In my experience, **code review is the most effective way to get tests**. You tell the team that code changes must be reviewed before they are accepted into the shared build. Then, you check the contributions, and if they need related tests, you ask for the tests.

Some of the people on your team will be enthusiastic about testing, and they become your enforcers. You can do it in pairs, where each person reviews code from his or her assigned buddy. This is like pair programming, but a lot more efficient. Other approaches include asking tech leads to review code from their contributing team members and setting up group code reviews with voting.

Assembla offers features to help you with any of these review mechanisms.

Test-driven development

In test driven development, before writing code developers write tests for it, as a sort of specification. This process gives you a lot of automated tests. You will find that some people in your organization have patience for this process. They will argue that the slow pace of this process is more than offset by the increase in quality that comes from thinking through logical requirements and writing them down as tests. Others in your organization will strongly disagree. I recommend going back to code review as a way to resolve this issue.

Outsourcing to QA

You can send the responsibility for making automated tests to a QA professional or team. This is a good way to free up your developers, if you have a regression testing framework that is designed for QA people.

However, outsourcing to QA can introduce some inefficiency. Because the QA guys are paid to make tests, they are often slow to notice when the tests aren't finding problems, or require a lot of rework.

Code coverage?

Some developers will apply pressure for maximum code coverage. Code coverage is the percentage of lines of code that run when you run automated tests. I am not sure if it is an important measure. If a change breaks something, it usually breaks multiple tests. You can have limited code coverage and still find enough problems to shorten your testing period and give developers confidence to make changes. To get started, you can write tests only for bugs that get reported. Since bugs cluster together in evolving or difficult code, this strategy will find many errors with a limited number of tests.

Testing Topologies

Where do you test your code? You probably use one of the following topologies.

Release candidate or centralized

The release candidate strategy is used by most software projects, and it is a required part of the iterative release pattern and the mainline CI pattern. Contributors build the latest version of their code into a "release candidate," then test it with manual and automated testing. Then they fix bugs and make another release candidate. They do this until there are no more important bugs. At that time they release the candidate.

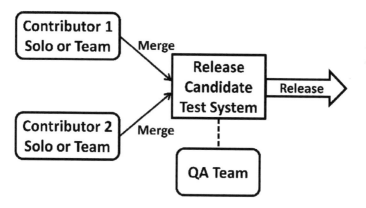

Benefits: This is a very efficient pattern. You only have one version to test. Manual testers know where to find it. You only need one automated test system.

Problems: As you add code and have more things to test, it takes longer and longer to test and stabilize the release candidate. This release candidate method will not get you continuous release, because you can assume there will be problems when you merge multiple changes that haven't been tested together.

If you add "centralized" continuous integration to the release candidate, you get this workflow:

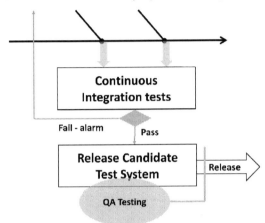

Developer or pre-commit

Developers can test code and run automated tests on their own workstations. This "pre-commit" testing is often required before committing code to a centralized continuous system.

After testing locally, team members can send their changes to other developers who can test it on their workstations. This is the mainstay of the "maintainer" model of development used by many open source and mobile projects.

Benefits: This is always a first step. It works without an automated test server. It scales with the number of developers. It can be used to review and clean up code that is contributed to a mainline continuous process.

Problems: Developers do not always run automated tests. When they do run tests, it takes time. Maintainers can fall behind in testing and code review, and when there are problems they may not respond promptly to contributors. Maintainers have to do manual work to start automated tests.

Multiple test systems / Distributed

A process with multiple test systems is more complicated, but also a lot more scalable. Every contributing team or major feature has its own test system. Developers should be able to get these systems on demand from a cloud platform to test major changes. The test systems run automated tests, and also provide a place for QA and Story Owners to go and help with testing.

Benefits: Multiple test systems can accommodate a large number of contributions without slowing down the final test and release cycle. They can get you to continuous release with an "as late as possible" integration strategy, in which a change is released before it hits problems caused by other changes.

Problems: Multiple test systems are complicated to set up and maintain. Testers need to learn to act as consultants, helping developers who ask them to look at specific test systems.

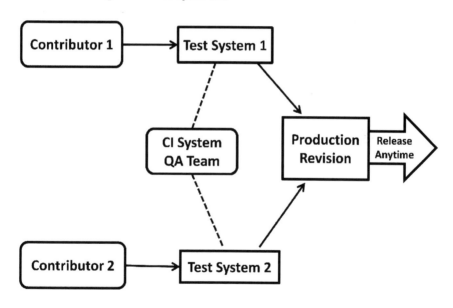

Test review branches or merge requests

With Gerrit or Assembla protected branches, you can put each change into a temporary branch with a merge request. The automated test system will see the branch and run tests on it. This pattern automates the process of making a new test environment for each change. It can deliver clean code to a centralized continuous process.

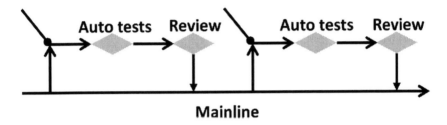

Benefits: Test review branches are very clean. Reviewers do not review code until it passes automated tests. All code that reaches the mainline has been tested.

Problems: Test review branches are complicated to set up and maintain.

I believe that this system of putting changes into branches for test and review obsoletes the older patch-based and "pre-commit" review systems. It is much easier to apply automated testing to real branches. There are fewer steps for developers who want to test, review and comment. And, if reviewers want to fix the contribution, it is easy for them just to put a new change in the review branch.

Product Management

Three Challenges

Product managers (a title from product companies) and product owners (a title from Agile teams) decide what features go into a product, and what those features look like. I am going to use the term "PO" or "product owner."

It's not important to build something. It's important to build the RIGHT thing. We know that this is a difficult problem because MOST software features are wrong. Users ignore them. You can do a lot of work and get no value. The product owner gives meaning to the work of everyone else on the team by making products that are meaningful to users.

Product owners are dealing with three big shifts:

1) Batch -> Continuous

The job used to be easier. In the old days, product owners had enough time to do their work because development was ... slow. They were often waiting for developers to finish the last batch of requests. However, developer productivity has increased dramatically from year to year and decade to decade. When you crank up your continuous Agile team, the situation will be completely reversed. Developers will be waiting for the PO. A full-speed continuous delivery development team can run over the product owners and leave feature roadkill.

2) Strategy -> Measurement

When you move to continuous delivery, strategy becomes less important, because you have more ways to get immediate feedback. For example, you can measure what users actually do. That is more accurate than what they say they want. Therefore the product owner has a responsibility to set up measurements, and after changes are released, loop back to analyze their impact.

3) Requirements -> User Experience

Your measurements will be strongly affected by usability. Usability, and the careful stewardship of scarce user attention, is the main battlefield on which most products are fighting now. You will need to understand usability in theory and practice, and measure it. You may find that requirements gathering becomes less important. A product can die if requirements get too far ahead of usability.

Measure

Data gives you power. You can argue for months about the value of a particular feature. If you bring in measurements that show how people use the feature, you can win the argument in a few seconds.

The power is within your grasp. If you run an online service, your machines are collecting a stream of big data, sometimes very big. They are logging speed and capacity usage, errors, transactions, completed purchases, dropoff rates, bounce rates. The DevOps motto is "measure everything."

We found that most product managers throw most of this data away.

Double your capacity

According to Microsoft product CTO Adam Pisoni, "What you realize when you begin to be very data-driven is a very large percentage of our ideas are bad." Measurements help you find the good ideas.

Users pay attention to fewer than half of the features and feature changes that developers add to software. If you can figure out which features they are ignoring, and also ignore those features, you can double your development capacity at no extra cost. Actually, you double your effective capacity for everything related to product releases — product management, development, and marketing.

Watch what users do, and NOT what they say. You can't rely on user surveys to figure out which features user want, because users tend to ask for more features than they actually use. They also ask for bad features. They have limited imaginations. As a product developer, it's your job to transform those bad feature requests into good features, using your special skills, in-depth understanding of the innovation landscape, creativity, and measurements.

The extra features that users ask for can damage your product because of a strange psychological effect that I call "averaging down." When you add an unfinished feature to a high quality application, users will notice it and "average down" their opinion of the quality of the application. Even if they never use the feature, they will be less likely to recommend the application.

Test with feature flags

The unveil process gives you many opportunities to test the usability and usefulness of new features. You can use feature flags to show changes to your own team, or to specific users. You can use feature flags to do A/B testing, where you show changes to a subset of your users (group B) and see if they show any difference in feedback or usage patterns compared with group A.

Test pricing

Users are especially untruthful when you ask them about the price they are willing to pay. They will always ask you to underprice your product, which is the same thing that I would do if you asked me. They complain loudly at the price points that will make you the most money. If they weren't ready to buy, they would not bother to complain. You should test your pricing with new package offers, and make pricing decisions based on the amount of money you collect from actual purchases. For inspiration, go to Starbucks and look at the way they are trying to get $4 for a new kind of coffee when their competitors are charging $1.50. I notice that these offers come and go, and sometimes they stick.

Get the data

Where is this data? If you run an online service, you already have a lot of data. You might be collecting it through services like NewRelic, which tracks server performance, errors, and usage so that you can keep your servers running. They call this "application performance monitoring." NewRelic has started re-using this data for product management, which they call "Software Analytics — Agile business insights from your app." That's what you can do with all of your data.

If your app has a mobile front end, or a partner API, you can log the API calls and report on them. You can also get packaged services that add local usage logging inside your mobile app. This data an important tool for improving engagement and usability, and the top competitors will all be doing it.

If you do online marketing, you probably have tools that follow the progress of users through Web sites and email, as they buy and don't buy. You can use the same tools to find out what they use and don't use.

Add your own logging. You should be streaming important events into some sort of database table where you can do manual or automated reporting. You can turn on the native logging for your software platform. You can enhance the logs to include key information about the user or the subscriber. It's worth the effort.

If your product is installed on the user's computer, you have a difficult challenge. Your attempts at rapid development and data-driven product management will be frustrated by the fact that you don't know what the users are doing, or even if they installed the newest version. In some cases, you may wait a year or more to get feedback from a big enough installed base. Don't let this continue! Add usage data logging to your product. At strategic times, ask for permission to send this data home. Ask to send data home by default, and let users turn the option off. If the system (or the user) detects an error, ask for permission to send data home.

Recently I installed a touchpad that came with a driver. It watched me for a few weeks. Only then did it pop up a message asking to send usage data home and asking me for a product review. It was smart enough to ask AFTER it saw that I was happily and proficiently using the device — a very strategic time.

MVP for Fun and Profit

If you can measure user reactions, you can build an MVP. "Minimum Viable Product," or MVP, is a phrase from Eric Reis and his Lean Startup book. An MVP is a product or product improvement that it is just functional enough to test customer reaction. At the same time that you test your product, you can also test your business model and your ability to attract customers. The MVP can be as simple as an advertisement. You could advertise a product to see if people want it before you invest too much time developing it. You build the simplest product, or product change, that you can test for a measurable result.

It's a brilliant idea. It speeds up your product development, and it prevents you from wasting time.

However, in my opinion, MVP is really two ideas. There are two ways to improve your product. You can innovate, and you can optimize.

- You innovate when you give the customer something he didn't know he needed, or could get. Your creativity and ability to deliver go beyond the imagination of other market participants.

- After you innovate, you start to optimize. You incrementally improve your product and take it from useful, to good, to great. You can spend a lot of time making thousands of optimizations.

There are two related types of MVP, which I will call Mvp and mVP.

The MINIMUM viable product or product change is an optimization. You make small changes until you get measurable results. You reverse changes quickly if they aren't well received. You don't worry much about the impact of these tests on your reputation or other risks. You make changes frequently and don't worry about timing. It's all about execution. If you are working on optimization, just do it, and pay attention to the measurements.

The minimum VIABLE PRODUCT is an innovation. You have to produce a complete product to show what is possible. It needs to be a good product.

Early roadmaps should be built around the minimum VIABLE PRODUCT. A minimum VIABLE PRODUCT takes a lot longer to produce than a MINIMUM viable product, and it requires thoughtfulness and constant risk management. Designing a minimum VIABLE PRODUCT is an art. You will need to work hard to understand the essence of your product, and get to early releases that truly are VIABLE and MINIMUM. If you design by committee, you will miss the essence of the innovation, and miss on VIABLE. If you follow your instincts, you will usually overbuild and miss on MINIMUM.

Using the user

Minimum Viable Product and your brand

Minimum viable product is a brilliant idea. However, there is a dark side. When you actually release an MVP, you are burning your brand value.

It's interesting that many of the people who are interested in the Minimum Viable Product approach are also fans of Apple products and Apple product strategy. Does Apple ever release an MVP? No. That would damage their brand. They release products that are streamlined, but fully designed and tested and packaged by fanatics for their intended use. That's why people feel good about using Apple products.

A Minimum Viable Product is by definition not a very good product. It's a product with annoying gaps. You want people to complain about those gaps. You want to find the gaps that are worth complaining about. You are not trying to give the user the best possible experience. You are using the user to help you design your product and business model.

A skilled user of the MVP concept conducts very brief tests, or tests with a small number of users. The tests are long enough to get useful feedback from user reactions, but not long enough to change the brand perception for the bulk of potential users.

Using the user

When you release a product for beta testing, you are not doing it for the benefit of the user. The product is likely to have bugs. It changes frequently. Just when the user is getting used to one behavior, you put in a different behavior. You are doing the release for the benefit of your developers. Your development team needs the feedback they get from the beta release, and they use it to make a better product. The users are serving the developers.

Using the user can be a good thing. It's an important resource for development, provided that you know when to do it and when to stop doing it.

If you are a business that offers free products or services, you can exploit the customers who use them. Those cheapskates owe you something. Hit them with MVP-style tests and changes. Minimize the damage by making the tests short, or exposing them to a subset of users. In a mature product, keep tests fast and small.

If you get good enough at this tactic, it becomes an efficient way to replace other types of testing. In an online system where you can do real-time release and rollback on multiple servers, you can push your changes to a few servers and watch the results.

When to flip

When a product is ready for full release, flip your priorities. The customer is always right, and the development team serves them.

When you are building a new product you are using three precious resources: time, money, and brand goodwill. As you try to make a better product, you will burn each of these resources in calculated amounts. You will make decisions about when to burn money and brand to drive development. You will do this as quickly as possible. You will make decisions about when to switch back, make money, and build brand value with consistent quality. Go forth and prosper.

Velocity and Quality

You can use the extra capacity and flexibility that you get from Continuous Agile to increase the speed with which you release changes (increase velocity), or you can use it to reduce the number of errors, crashes, and usability problems (increase quality). The PO will often be called on to balance the need for quality with the desire for velocity.

We can show the trade between quality (Q) and velocity (V) with the following chart.

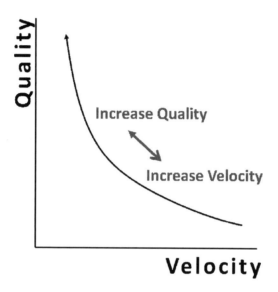

You can increase Q by reducing V and holding each feature longer for testing and improvement.

You can increase V by reducing Q and finding more problems in parallel. This is the "using the user" tactic. In a continuous process, if you force releases out with some problems, you will find and fix problems faster.

As quality increases, velocity decreases. This explains why companies try to hold products in "beta" for a long time. They can get away with lower quality, and it increases their velocity.

Quality typically improves during the life cycle of a software project. We can divide this chart into some quality bands that show stages in the lifecycle of the software.

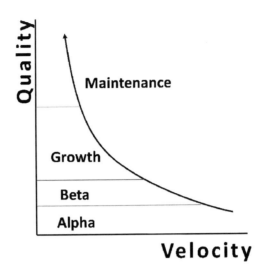

As a product manager, you don't have much influence on this curve over the short term. It is set by your team and your process. However, you can move on the curve by setting quality standards. You can allow releases with increased quality and decreased velocity, or decreased quality and increased velocity. You can set quality standards by deciding to release to audiences with different quality requirements - alpha, beta, and full. You will get to market faster, with a higher quality product, if you know when to switch. You should not do it too late, because you will waste time to market. But, you should not do it too early because you will slow down development.

One paradox

The fastest way to increase Q is to increase V. To increase V, you decrease Q. So, you decrease Q to increase Q. Then, you find and fix problems faster, and Q increases faster.

The lesson of this paradox is that you should not try to move to quickly out of beta quality, to high quality. This will kill your velocity and delay your project. This is a classic mistake from a mature team with high quality standards or high risk aversion. To make this team feel better about releasing with lower quality, you should give them options to release to smaller "beta" type audiences.

Economists call this type of chart an "efficient frontier." You can be inside the line, with worse quality and/or velocity - just stop paying attention. But, it is unlikely that you will get outside of the line. That is why you lower velocity when you insist on increased quality.

Consider the following chart.

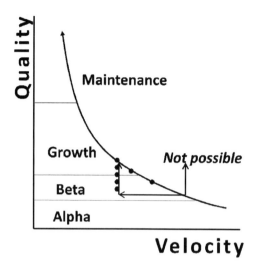

In the picture above we use monthly dots show two possible paths for the product. In one world, the software travels up the quality-velocity curve and gets safely out of beta quality after about three months. In the second world, we have strong quality enforcers. They make changes (like holding back releases) that reduce velocity and also reduce the speed of finding problems. They want to increase quality with the same velocity, but this is not possible. If the team is working efficiently, they can only make changes that reduce velocity. So, it takes them 5 months to get to the same place.

How to increase quality AND velocity

The long-term solution is to improve your process so that it has higher quality at every velocity. **You cannot do this by adding QA people.** QA people will find problems, rather than eliminate them. You can do it by improving other layers of your development process:

- Frequent full releases to flush out problems

- Monitoring and measurement and feedback directly to developers

- Automated testing, and more layers of automated testing

- Engaged story owners

Learn Before Launch

You can reduce stress and produce a better product if you separate "release" from "launch." Release as frequently as possible, with a small unveil process. Measure and learn. Then, when you have everything that you need to make a statement in the marketplace, do a bigger launch.

The role of releases

Releases are what developers do to deliver new features to EXISTING users. Releases should go out as frequently as possible.

Some releases are so incremental that they might not have very much impact on the way that users think about the product. Some users will be happy because they are waiting for new features. Some users will notice improvements. We will watch some users as test subjects, and measure their usage of new features. We will ask some users for feedback and testimonials that we can use in launch promotions.

Some releases are hidden for a majority of users, waiting for a bigger unveil.

The role of launches

"Launch" is what the marketing and/or training people do, after the release, to show it to NEW users, and create IMPACT in the marketplace. Impact will be increased if the release has big themes and new capabilities. Launches should happen when the product is ready.

Massive stress reduction

Many software producers will set a date to release a new product, and schedule a launch on that same date, with meetings and training and marketing activities. Software companies can be ripped apart by this process. It is a destructive pattern. It creates a lot of stress for the development team, because they can never be sure that they will have a good product on the pre-determined date. It creates a lot of stress for the marketing team and senior management. They schedule expenditures and media and meetings around the release date. However, they do not actually know when the release will be ready. They go into a frenzy of prioritization and micro-management as the date approaches.

You can get massive stress reduction if you learn before launch. In the new system, you will wait until all of the key features are released. You do not need to unveil them to all users. THEN, when you can see that everything looks good, you plan your launch.

Confidence

You will want to have confidence that your development team will rapidly deliver the product you want, without the pressure of a fixed release date. You will gain this confidence if you see their work in frequent releases. Releases must be frequent and they should get shown on a daily, weekly, or monthly schedule.

If you have confidence that your product will be great, you will not be in a hurry to launch. You will be able to wait until you are fully ready to make an impact. You will understand that the goal is not to launch. The goal is to launch a great product.

Product Management

Unblock!

When the development team gets going fast enough, they start to implement stories that product owners have never refined, or even approved, and they produce features you do not want. This will make the developers uncomfortable. They don't want to be criticized for building the wrong thing. They want to bask in the glory of building the right thing. They will start to demand better product management, better stories, better design guidance. You must rise to the challenge.

Furthermore, you must do it without blocking the developers. We are going to unblock them so that after we give them an acceptable story to work on, they can work at full speed and release. We are going to move to one piece flow where we manage one feature - one story - at a time. The product owner has a responsibility to ride this process through to the end.

At Assembla, we have renamed the role "story owner." The story owner is responsible for taking stories from use cases, to design, to development, to release, to internal testing and refinement, to the big "unveil", and then to measurement.

Traditionally, the product owner started with product strategy and requirements: a study of the market, user needs, and user requirements. This is still important input. However, I think of strategy and requirements as a team sport. If you are releasing frequently, a lot of feedback about user needs reaches a lot of people in your organization. To manage this we use an "Epic" planning process, where different stakeholders can keep a list of the stories that they need, and move them through to development.

The Prioritized Backlog

All Agile processes rely on a prioritized backlog. This is a list of implementation tasks or "stories," sorted so that the tasks that should be worked on next are on the top.

The first job of a product owner is to make sure there are items on top of the backlog that are ready for implementation. They need to be important, and they need to be fully defined as stories with use cases.

When you start a project, you build the backlog with "roadmapping." You brainstorm about all of the things that you want to do, and then you sort them so that the tasks or stories on the top represent a minimum useful release.

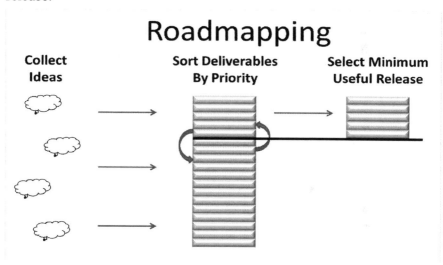

Roadmapping

| Collect Ideas | Sort Deliverables By Priority | Select Minimum Useful Release |

In a continuous process, you "pull" tasks off the backlog when you are ready to work on them, like this:

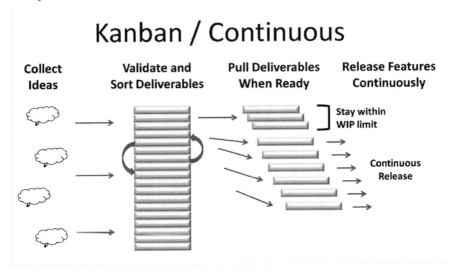

In a distributed process, the backlog should always be represented in an online ticketing or issue tracking system. That way everyone on the team can see the items on the top of the list and discuss them.

Epics and Allocations

If you have more than 20 items on the backlog, you will find it very hard to sort them by priority. You will naturally start to divide the backlog into topics, or into an outline-style project plan. An excellent way to handle this is to treat each important topic as an "epic" - a list of stories to implement a major deliverable.

Epics and stories

Epic owners will select the high value deliverables to become "work in progress." They incrementally pull stories out of an epic, one at a time, and move them to your sprint backlog or work in progress.

A story is something that you can release at one time. You can put a story on the backlog, pull it for implementation, release it, and close it. An epic cannot be released at one time, because it contains multiple stories that are released at different times.

You will find it annoying if you put epics into the backlog list, or on the cardwall for current work in progress. They will hang there for a long time and always look stuck. In a lean, continuous system, you do not ever want to be stuck. Epics should go into a different view in your planning system.

You will want to divide your epics into small stories and build them incrementally. This will reduce stress, because you can use continuous delivery. It will reduce bugs, because it is easier to find problems in a small change with fewer lines of code. It will force you to identify the highest value deliverables, so that you can work on them first.

Hierarchy

For example, my top level job today is Assembla content marketing. One of my major deliverables is an eBook about continuous delivery. I will build this incrementally, with help from a Web designer and my friends. I will show each chapter as it emerges. My planning hierarchy would look something like this:

Assembla content marketing (Top level stakeholder)

- Write an ebook about continuous delivery (Epic level)

    ○ Create a style sheet and HTML design (Story level)

    ○ Write the table of contents (Story level)

    ○ Write the introduction (Story level)

    ○ Write the "About Agile" chapter (Story level)

Organizing around epic owners

You can organize the top level of your outline in various ways. If you are a professional services company, you will want to put major customer accounts at the top level. If you are an enterprise IT shop, you will put line of business leaders or other "stakeholders" at the top level. If you are a software product company, you will probably end up with an organization something like this:

Strategic product development (owned by the CEO and product managers)

- Feature your CEO really cares about

- Feature your product owners know that users want

Architecture and technical debt (owned by the CTO)

- Something your developers know they need

Bugs (owned by customer support)

- Bug fixes demanded by users or by automated logging

- Stories that the customer support team knows will reduce support calls

Marketing and funnel (owned by marketing)

- Improvements to the startup process to get users to sign up or refer other users (Marketing guys should be ready to serve as story owners for these requests)

These topics are not all the same type. Some of them are very specific changes, like bugs. Some of them are defined around a bigger issue or around a team. However, each top-level topic has someone who cares about it deeply. The support team needs to reduce bugs and support calls. The marketing team needs selling tools built into the product.

When you organize this way, each top level category, and each epic, will have an owner, someone who really cares about that epic.

Allocation of effort

Here is the trick that makes an enterprise planning process work.

Once you have organized your outline this way, you are ready to create your ordered backlog for the implementers. You don't have to order everything. You only need to select and order the next 20 items.

Since all of the epic owners care about what they are doing, it will be a big mess if you invite all of them to a meeting, let them lobby for their personal epics, and expect a product owner to select a small number of important items that will make everyone happy. Now it becomes clear why it is difficult to sort more than 20 items.

But decision-making is easy if we allocate a fixed number of stories to each epic owner. Let them choose X stories they can have in the backlog and in work in progress. In the example above, we might say that the CEO and new product team get 8 stories, the support team gets 4 stories, the marketing team gets 4 stories, and the developers and architects get 4 stories.

You can do this allocation in a batch, where everyone picks their stories at the same time. Or you can do it continuously, and allow epic owners to pick new stories when existing ones are finished.

This type of allocation is a central feature of enterprise planning frameworks like Scaled Agile Framework, Disciplined Agile Delivery, and Enterprise Agility. It is often called "Portfolio Allocation," because you are allocating capacity to a portfolio of projects.

Some team leaders will agree with Joel Spolsky that a software team backlog or cardwall should not be bigger than 20 items. This is a good way to maintain clarity for an implementation team. However, it is an extremely naive way to think about project planning. We send men to the moon and put three billion people onto a mobile network. We don't do those things 20 tasks at a time. The 20 task limit is not a natural limit for projects. It is a function of human psychology, the longest list that one human can reliably sort into priority order.

In contrast, with epic planning we can use many people to coordinate a more complicated project. With allocations, we can maintain clarity by sending stories to implementation teams in batches of 20 or fewer.

The Story Owner Process

We use a "story owner" role to design and deliver great features in a continuous delivery process. This replaced the traditional idea of a product owner or product manager. A story owner is responsible for delivering one great feature at a time.

The story owner takes a story (a feature for a user) from initial definition of the story, through build, test, release, announcement and measurement. Here is a picture of what a story owner does at Assembla.

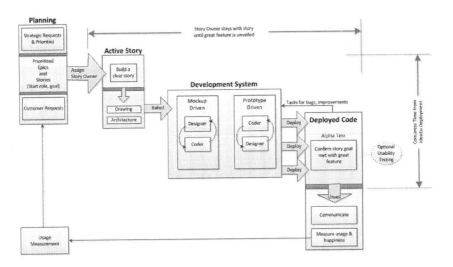

Lean tricks

We used some lean tricks to make this work:

- **One-piece flow**. One-piece flow is the lean idea that you should be able to make and delivery one piece (for example, one car) rather than building in big batches. A story owner pulls one story, explains the story with use cases, works to design it, program it, test it, and release it to customers.

- **Un-waterfall**. When trying to satisfy developer needs for good, stable use cases, we were tempted to go to a waterfall-type process where we would commit to a story, then make a design, then start development. That would have been bad! To make a great feature, we need to have some discovery and improvement while we are building. Story owners only need to get agreement that they have a clear, useful, important user story before they dive into implementation. This means that most of the story owner work is going to be inside the development and release process.

- **Unblock developers**. We don't want developers waiting around for batch processes like planning and releases. Once they commit to working with a story owner on a story, they start releasing to their test systems. As soon as they think something is ready to try, they push it through to production release, with no approval required from the story owner.

- **Hide, then unveil**. The developer can release a feature whenever he or she wants, but that doesn't mean it is ready for customers. We use flags to hide it. This gives the story owner a chance to try the feature in test systems, test usability in various ways, and even turn it on for beta users. During this time we're still inside the development cycle for the story, so the developers and designers are still helping to improve it. When it's ready, and we're ready to explain it to customers, the story owner does an "unveil." We show it to everyone, post on the blog, adjust tutorials, and send emails announcing the new feature.

The Story Owner Checklist

Find story owners

Product managers at Assembla MUST be good story owners. We use this idea to guide our recruiting and training. Every product manager must start with the ability to design and deliver a great feature. An Assembla product manager must understand our product category well enough to be able to be a story owner for half of our features.

But we found that product managers were not enough. We needed to expand our capacity to do story owner work. The solution was to equip a wider range of people to do the work.

Story owners can be professional product owners, but they can also be developers or designers, or come from other roles such as customer service and marketing. Anyone who deeply understands the user and the use case is qualified.

Another exciting possibility is finding "guest story owners" - opinionated users or outside experts who drop in to work with the development team.

We think that newbies can be good story owners if we give them a guide or checklist for doing the work. The **Assembla Story Owner Checklist** is included below. You can use it as a guide for your own version.

Story owner responsibilities

A story owner should understand the USER of a feature. (It helps a lot if he or she IS a user.)

A story owner must be able to accept a story when it is not completely defined and be responsible for:

- Developing the story so that the goal is clear, adding information to explain it, removing details that are not required, and answering all questions about the story.

- Working with designers and developers to build the feature.

- Improving and finishing the beta version.

- Ensuring that usability is good.

- Releasing the feature to users, communicating with them, and measuring their reactions.

The story owner at work

The story owner has two primary goals for every new feature and significant improvement:

- Get the feature into full release as quickly as possible. It should not become stuck or overly complicated. Accelerated delivery increases the value of our work, because it eliminates partially-finished features that customers cannot use. It makes planning easier, because there are fewer features to track inside the implementation process. It makes development simpler, because developers can focus on a smaller number of tasks at one time.

- Make the feature a great one that people will use, and that users will be happy about. Continue to improve usability right up to the point where the feature is unveiled.

Story owners should work on a limited number of stories, no more than three. They have to finish one of those stories before they can begin work on a new one.

In the Assembla ticket system, a story can be represented by a ticket that is assigned to a story owner. We create subtasks for programming tasks, design tasks and bugs, and those can be assigned to different people. The subtasks go into the same milestone or sprint as the story (usually "Current"). That way, you can manage the backlog at the level of stories, but when you move a story in the current milestone or sprint, you can be assign and track the subtasks individually.

We have two different development paths. "Prototype-driven" stories start with the coding of a prototype version of the feature, which then gets design and usability improvements. "Mockup-driven" stories start with making improvements to a mockup, which then goes to development for implementation.

Developers can release features at any time, without waiting for approval from the story owner. They can use the continuous delivery process at full speed. They use QA and the story owner as consultants. However, new features have switches so that they are only visible to alpha users. The story owner controls the decision about when the new feature is unveiled for all other users.

Assembla's Story Owner Checklist

Story phase

Deliverable: An explanation of the way the feature will be used, and a description of the feature that answers questions for developers and helps them make correct implementation decisions.

- Define the story with a clear role, goal and action
- Provide a user scenario or an example that shows why we need it.
- Expand (get ideas) and contract (prioritize and select the important aspects)
- Add drawings (if appropriate)
- Determine if we need any architecture decisions
- Describe acceptance tests to clarify all of the logical use cases

Building phase

Deliverable: A feature that works.

- Select Prototype- or Mockup-driven development. If the feature requires a significant architecture, start with a prototype. If the feature has a big user interface, start with a mockup. Otherwise, if you are developer, start with a prototype, if you are designer, start with a mockup, and if you are a product manager, marketer or guest, start with whichever process seems easiest for you.
- Prevent unnecessary requirements and complexity by determining if feature and architecture additions are really required for the user story. Often, they are not.
- If you need architecture work (new data structures, object structures, or server process flow), create a subtask, and ask ONE person to make an architecture proposal. This proposal should be discussed and approved by the architecture team.
- Create subtasks to assign design and development work
- Answer all questions from team members within a few hours
- After a prototype, move the story into design. After a mockup, move the story into programming

- Create a subtask if you need to assign programming or design work

- Arrange for a staging server where you can test the changes

- Release features with alpha switches to control the unveil process

Finishing phase

Deliverable: A feature that makes a lot of users happy.

- Test the feature. Check usability.

- Gather feedback. Interview users. Conduct usability tests with untrained users.

- If improvements are required, post new tasks for each bug or improvement.

- Manage the unveil process to turn on the feature for all users

- Communicate the use cases and benefits to users through the appropriate use of in-app announcements, blog posts, posts on community forums, and emails

- Define metrics and measure usage and user happiness

- Determine if additional refinement is required, or if the story can be closed

Stories

A story describes a change or feature that you can move through to a single release. A story is a useful concept for any Agile process, including continuous Agile. Your developers will be much more effective if you give them good stories.

We write stories down in an online ticket or issue tracking system. This gives us a place to discuss the story, sometimes in great detail. We can look at the ticket to see who is working on it, what code changes are related to it, and where the changes are in the code contribution process.

Stories and tasks

Stories will often have implementation tasks attached to them. They may also be an element of an epic, or of an even higher level topic. The full planning hierarchy is:

- Top level stakeholder
  - Epic
    - Story
      - Task

It is a good practice to do your backlog planning and estimating with epics and stories, but hold off on expanding the stories with implementation tasks until you are ready to pull them off the backlog and start work.

Make a new implementation task if you think a new developer or designer or tester can pull it.

When you post bug reports for a story, post a new task ticket for each bug. Then you can test and close one bug at a time without being confused by other issues in a long discussion thread.

Required information

Traditionally, a story has the structure "As <a persona>, I want to <product functionality/action>, so that <benefit/goal>." For example, "As a reader of this eBook, I want to see a NEXT: link on the bottom of every page, so that I can move to the next page without constantly scrolling back to the menu."

You should include:

- A role (Persona) of the user

- A goal: What am I trying to do when I use this feature? Why?

- An action: The action is the feature description. It is a way of reaching the goal.

Now, **combine them into a use case or a user scenario**. This is where you really tell a story. Pick a real or close-to-real person to represent the persona. Provide an example of how this person is using the system. Give real example(s) in a full paragraph. This helps others on the team understand the user's perspective and situation. If we agree on the use case, we are free to be creative in how we design and develop.

Never send a story to developers without a clear description of the user and use case.

If you are defining a new feature, you will be tempted to expand it with many new ideas. But too many ideas make a story that is difficult to design and deliver. Before you go to implementation, find the element that has the most value. Shrink the story by taking out everything that you do not need.

Optional information

If you have a solid use case, you can forward the story for design and development. You don't want to block the design process. You want design to be a process of discovery and flow. However, if you have additional information, you should add it to the story. Here are some of the types of information that are useful.

Feature description.

If you know what the action will look like, describe it.

Implementation tasks.

If you know the steps to implement, list them. This will help when the story is expanded into a list of implementation tasks.

Drawings, storyboards and mockups

Make a quick sketch, or print out and mark up a screen to show how to implement the action. Snap a picture of a whiteboard or a pencil sketch, or export a wireframe from a drawing or presentation program. A storyboard is a flowchart showing the steps or screens for the action. A mockup is a complete picture of the feature in HTML or PowerPoint form. But do not create a final mockup. At this stage we want clarity, but not perfection.

Architecture and architecture questions

Include an architecture discussion if there are changes to data structures, or UI libraries, or data objects, or server processes. If there is a question about architecture, assign a single developer to make an architecture proposal, because group discussions rarely deliver a good architecture.

Acceptance test cases

Most features have many logical use cases. If you write specific tests for each case, it will be easy for developers to produce correct features without a lot of iterations. This can save you time in both development and testing.

Beta and post-release tests

List feedback expected from the normal beta test, and information required beyond that. What measurable changes are we expecting? How can we check those?

Unveiling

Who will we release to first? List any specific unveiling plans or conditions.

More Than One Way to Design

There is always more than one correct way to design something. In our case, we make Web software, and our story owners can decide if they want a prototype process or a mockup process.

Prototype process: The developer creates a prototype and works on it until we know we have the right functionality, then we ask a designer to make it look good.

Mockup process: We start by creating a nice design and an HTML mockup, then ask a programmer to implement it.

Build Phase

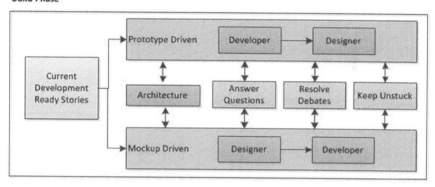

I recommend choosing the process that looks easiest. If you are developer, start with a prototype. If you are designer, start with a mockup. If you are a product manager, a marketer, or a guest, start with the easiest next step.

However, there are two reasons you might make the choice based on the feature. If the feature requires a significant architecture, start with a prototype. If the feature has a big user interface, start with a mockup.

Distributed Teams

Co-located, Outsourced, Distributed

Co-located

In the beginning, software teams were co-located. Everyone sat in the same room, met frequently, pored over papers and blackboards, and discussed their plans. In those days, offices were a lot bigger so that everyone would be in the same place. I remember huge cube farms at the now extinct Digital Equipment Corporation.

Meeting in-person is still the preferred option for most managers, and many team members. Scrum-based Agile methodologies will always recommend that you work in co-located teams. That is one of the major weaknesses of Scrum. Most startups will try to pull all of their team members into one location. This reduces design time, but increases recruiting time.

Outsourced

An "outsourced" team is a co-located team that is in a different location from your main project planners. Outsourcers like to organize complete teams in their home cities. However, you don't need to hire outsourcers to get this topology. Any large organization or large project will have teams in multiple locations.

An outsourced team tends to be managed like a co-located team. Each co-located team has a specific area of responsibility or expertise. The team expertise can be functional - for example, "QA" or "Hardware." However, an Agile team will try to be cross-functional and divide the work so that each team delivers a complete product or feature. In this type of organization, there is often a fairly awkward movement of work between teams, described as "throwing something over the wall."

Distributed

A distributed team does not throw work over the "wall" between teams and specialties. It tears down the wall so that a person in any location can participate in any of the work that is required. It is organized as a single global team.

Your teams may become distributed because:

- You want to work with someone with special skills in another location.

- A member of your team moves to a remote location or works at home for family reasons.

- You have outsourced teams that you want to reorganize into true distributed teams.
- You want to solve your talent shortage by recruiting globally.
- You already work in a global corporation.

I have rarely been on a conference call with my customers at SAP that didn't include people on at least three continents.

Co-located teams are a luxury. They allow us to use our habitual management and communications skills. However, distributed teams are a necessity. It has been a long time since I have seen a large team that is completely co-located, and today I rarely see even small co-located teams. We can design our Agile process to unblock these teams and make them productive. And, because we have access to more and better talent, they will ultimately be more productive than our old co-located teams.

A truly distributed, single global team is the most flexible and scalable way to organize continuous delivery.

Communications

Your distributed team will need communication tools and techniques to replace the in-person chatter of a co-located team.

Skip the conference call

Do not try to manage your distributed project with daily conference calls. People hate it. Think about a project where you participated in a lot of long conference calls. Did you enjoy it? Was it a satisfying, successful project? I have asked hundreds of people this question and they have never recalled a case of a good project with a lot of conference call time. I find that conference calls are a good indicator of failing projects. They make the boss feel better by allowing him or her to share his or her problems. They don't solve problems for team members. They eat time that could be used to fix problems. They come at awkward times of the day. I laugh when I hear about how the boss has to get up in the middle of the night to inflict a conference call on his Asian team. Calls demand attention, and attention is a very scarce commodity.

Synchronous versus asynchronous

"Synchronous" communications happen between two or more people at the same time. Face-to-face conversations are synchronous. Telephone calls are synchronous. In "asynchronous" communications, people can respond at different times, at their convenience. Emails and text messages are asynchronous communications.

A naive manager will try to replace his co-located conversations with equivalent, high-bandwidth, synchronous communications. This leads to a lot of conference calls, some of them late at night. It also leads to a vision of the future where everyone is in front of a camera, video-conferencing with colleagues as if they were at the next desk or in front of the proverbial water cooler.

However, many hard-working people prefer asynchronous communication. Even if they are sitting at the next desk, you will see that they often email each other and respond at leisure. This trend is particularly strong among young people who prefer to receive text messages rather than voice calls.

Why do they prefer short and seemingly unsatisfying text messages over real conversations with friends and colleagues? There are two reasons. First, they don't want to be interrupted. They want to pay attention to the thing in front of them, which is often computerized. Second, they are multitasking, having many different conversations at one time. At the same time that you are trying to talk to them about a weekly plan (bla bla bla) they are discussing an engineering point they care about, and arranging for beers with friends.

As we become more productive, and as the competition for our attention intensifies, we come to prefer asynchronous communications. Also, we get annoyed by people who demand our attention for synchronous meetings.

Ticket and issue tracking systems

Write your ideas, requests, bug reports, and comments in an online ticket system. They will be visible to the entire team, and you have a running, long-term record of contributions.

If you are writing feature requests, learn to present complete "stories." That makes the implementation work easier, and you will get better results. We describe the elements of a good story in the Product Management chapter.

Your team will have a default view of the Work in Progress tasks which shows the status of each task, and shows who is working on it, or where it is waiting. Agile teams call this an "information radiator." You can always go to this view to find something to work on.

A good online ticketing system with comments and attachments is a requirement for a distributed team.

Email

I live on email. I type thousands of words per day in email. However, it's a dangerous addiction. You should avoid using email for team communications. Information in an email thread is invisible for other team members. This creates work for you when you have to relay the information. When people email you details that are not important, they waste your time. When they email you information that is important, you need to repost it for the team, which wastes your time. Avoid becoming a human router. I recommend using email only if you are asking a personal question. If people send you information by email that they should be sharing, just ignore the information until they post it properly.

Chat

Every distributed team should have a chat running. People like chat because it can be synchronous when they want to have a real conversation, and asynchronous when they want to come back to it later. You want a persistent chat that team members can come back to at any time. You probably also want a searchable history so that you can find that URL someone posted last week. We use Skype. You can now get chat systems designed for programming teams.

Wiki and message boards

You will want to post your documentation and instructions on a Wiki. If you are inviting new people to join the project, you should take some time to document the setup and other instructions. Later you will want to document test, build, and deploy procedures.

You will want to post status reports, meeting summaries, and major questions on a message board. These tools aren't absolutely required, but they are helpful and they help move communication out of email and into more visible formats.

Other communications tools

Other useful communication and collaboration tools include:

Online standup reports. Your team can post "What I did" and "What I will do today" and "What I need" on a form. We built this form into Assembla. It only takes about one minute to post a daily report this way, so it saves a lot of time compared with other types of reporting. After that you can get on the team chat to discuss any questions or needs. It's very useful to read the "What I will do today" reports, because you will often see that people are working on things that are not very important. By asking them to work on higher priority items, you can blast through project obstacles.

@mentions. In some ticketing and collaboration systems, you can @mention teammates to draw their attention to your comment or question. They will get a link on their dashboard that goes directly to the discussion. This is a great way to collaborate and build a visible discussion.

Communicating with code

An effective distributed programming team communicates with code. In fact, many of the most successful distributed projects are open source projects that communicate almost entirely through the exchange and review of code.

Distributed teams should have either a daily build or a continuous build of code. This shared build communicates a lot about the state of the project, and it gives everyone, even non-programmers, a way to see current code and comment about it. If you want your distributed group to work together as a team, then you want everyone to be working on the same thing - the shared build.

Programming teams exchange code through their version control systems. Code management workflows can facilitate many types of communication:

- Comments on individual lines of code.

- Comments attached to merge requests, change requests, changelists, and other types of code contributions.

- Instructions about standards for style, documentation and test coverage.

- Voting and consensus-building around feature and architecture questions.

- Discussions among product managers, users and non-technical participants about contributions accepted and deployed in the shared build.

An important function of a project manager is to improve communications between team members. If your team communicates mostly with code, then a non-technical project manager will not be able to participate. That is why modern continuous projects use tech leads who can understand code.

About those calls ...

I like to do big full-team calls to kick off a project. This ensures that everyone on the team hears the same plan and the same goals. Your team will form around the goal. After that, I do calls that include only the correct people, the people that need to be on the call. They will appreciate the call if it is for them.

Some teams are getting good results with Google Hangouts, which is a sort of informal, low-fidelity group video conferencing tool. It works better than a formal videoconference that requires a lot of setup and synchronous attention.

Things Teams Should Do

We find that a distributed team can become Agile and successful by doing a few simple things.

Write it down in tickets

If you have a feature request, or you want a developer or administrator to do something, or you have a comment about design or implementation or architecture, **write it down in a ticket**. To keep track of these notes in tickets you need a ticketing system (sometimes called an issue manager or bug tracker). You can then arrange the tickets into iterations or milestones with release dates. If you write down the information, everyone on the team can see it. The necessary people will be informed, and will make their contribution, without much effort on your part. It's magic.

On the other hand, you will get into trouble if you communicate requests one-on-one in phone or email or chat conversations. Those receiving the information will have to make an extra effort to forward it to others. The information may be lost, or communicated inaccurately. You may be forced to step in and act as a human hub, forwarding lots of emails to lots of people, and searching through your email threads for individual answers. Don't fall into this trap. Write everything down in a shared ticketing system, and have a good life.

Obstacle: Some people just will not move off email or conference calls. **Answer:** Stop enabling them. Refuse to forward their requests.

Share a daily or continuous build

If your team is distributed, you need to make sure that everyone is working on the same thing. That's what makes a blob of people into a team. You can ensure this coordination with a daily build: a version of the software that everyone can look at and test. Or you can go further and run continuous integration, so that you always have a current build that is shared.

Obstacle: You don't have good automated build scripts. **Answer:** This can be a hard technical problem, but automated build scripts are well worth the investment.

Obstacle: Some people don't want to show their work every day. They want to finish a complicated task, and then present it. They don't commit their code. **Answer:** Most work can be revealed incrementally. Divide the work into new stages, such as planning, mockup, etc. Use stimulus-response: if a developer waits a long time and commits a big feature, immediately find all of the problems with the feature and complain about them all at once. Then ask for fixes on a daily basis.

Daily standup report and chat

We like a lot of things about the Scrum methodology, including the daily stand up meeting where each team member says "What did I do, what will I do, what I need," followed by a short discussion. You can collect this information daily from each of your team members (we have a handy Standup tool in Assembla for this). When your team is forming, you should gather most of your team members together for a 10 minute chat to set priorities and answer "what I need" questions. We use Skype chat or Assembla chat.

Obstacle: Meetings take too much time. **Answer:** Team members should fill out the online form before starting the chat, so that in the chat people only answer questions and help with needs and obstacles. If this drags on, you can do other work while the chat is running.

Obstacle: Too many time zones. **Answer:** Pick a time that is survivable for everyone, and stick to it. People adapt to something that is consistent.

Once your team is running smoothly, you can skip the scheduled chat and keep a persistent chat that you use as needed throughout the day.

Meet or chat at a fixed time

I have seen Agile experts recommend moving around the time of a daily or weekly meeting or chat so that people in India will have an inconvenient time in one meeting, and people in America will have an inconvenient time in the next meeting. It sounds like a reasonable way to share the pain, but actually it is a very bad idea. The people who recommend this are the same people who complain that managing distributed Agile teams is too hard. They are sabotaging their own projects. You will find that when you move the time, people miss the meeting. If you keep the same time every day or every week, people will adapt to it. They will fit it into their lives, they will attend more reliably, and over time it will become more convenient for them. Meet or chat at the same time every day.

Also, when you discuss or post times, post the 24 hour time (18:00, not 6:00 pm). Also, post the UTC time as well as the time for the majority of team members. Assembla will show an individual's local time, and Google calendar will translate a time to the local time zone.

Provide a team activity stream

Our gregarious kids use the Facebook newsfeed: a stream of alerts on the Facebook home page that shows them what their friends are doing. They don't have to be in the same room to feel connected to each other. The same tactic is very important for uniting a distributed team. With the right web tool you can see the work of the team in real time. You should be able to see new tickets, ticket comments, code commits, questions, and build results. We have made the "Stream" a core feature of Assembla. It shows work as it is submitted, collects events from internal tools and external systems, and makes them available by Web, email, and RSS. Your team will be united by a visible activity stream. You will see teamwork, which is much better and easier to manage than task execution by individuals.

Obstacle: Our current tools don't support an activity stream. **Answer:** Get a tool that provides this visibility.

Recruit good people

Good people are the most important ingredient of any successful endeavor. This is especially true in software projects, where the productivity differences can be huge. If you are stuck with a co-located team you might not have much scope to improve individual productivity. However, a distributed team can recruit globally and look for the best and most appropriate people available in the world. Once you figure out how to manage a distributed team, you have no excuse not to recruit ambitiously.

Obstacle: You feel you can't manage remote team members. **Answer:** Do the first six things in this section of the guide, then come back to this one.

Obstacle: Relationships. You usually find people and outsourcers through recommendations from your friend's cousin. **Answer:** Try advertising. You might like it. Your friend's cousin doesn't draw from a very big pool of candidates.

Release on schedule

Agile teams should get releases out to users on a fixed schedule, frequently, ideally every day. This has a number of benefits. You get regular feedback from users, so you can improve your product rapidly. You fix bugs before each release, so quality stays high. And you establish credibility that you WILL deliver frequent releases, which reduces pressure on the development team and makes it easier to manage user requests.

As you approach your release date, you need to remove features that won't be completed, and stabilize the remaining features. This is very different from an approach that says you will release to users when you have finished the features. Do the release anyway. It builds your credibility. It also builds teamwork. The more frequently you release, the more frequently you bring everyone together to work on the same thing.

When people see these recommendations, they often say "That's a good idea, but..." and then raise obstacles. Let's provide answers to those obstacles.

Obstacle: Some users (or bosses) don't believe that they will get a follow-on release, so they insist on asking for EVERYTHING in the next release. If you let this happen, you will never get the release out. This is a self-reinforcing cycle, because if you don't release on time, they become even more sure that a release is a rare event, and they push even harder for "everything." **Answer:** Release on time. Users will start to believe they will get more releases, and they will not object if you move features to a follow-on release.

Obstacle: You just don't feel right about releasing unproven features to customers that expect sizzle and reliability. **Answer:** Do the release, but not to everyone. You can partition your user base into internal testers, beta testers, and risk-averse customers. Then target each release to the correct group.

Things Teams Should Skip

The definition of higher productivity is doing less work to get the same result. A task that you skip is a 100% productivity gain. This list contains unnecessary activities, and you can feel good when you stop doing them.

This list was originally called "Stick your con call up your estimate! 6 things you can skip to save time in a software project."

Travel

Travel takes a lot of time. You might think it speeds up projects by bringing your team together. However, if you know how to manage a distributed team it's actually a lot faster to sit down wherever you are and just do the work.

I like to have one big team meeting per year. This builds relationships between team members and gives us a chance to promote new ideas. You can have small meetings between the right people. I like to give team members a budget to travel and meet in small groups when they need or want a meeting to work on a specific question. They take advantage of this to go to nice places, and they get a lot of work done.

More project managers

We all know that bigger teams are slower. According to the statistics in the big fat book "Software Assessments and Best Practices" from Capers Jones, programmers are not responsible for this problem. Teams get slower when you add project managers. This is one reason that open source teams can scale up to do large projects. They are usually very flat with up to 20 contributors sending code to one maintainer, and everyone works on code. With good contributors and tech leads, you can do something similar.

Conference calls

I have noticed something when we go to "rescue" a project. If the team spends a lot of time on conference calls, the project is probably delayed. Maybe the delay causes the phone time. All I know is that conference call time is closely correlated with project failure. It's best to avoid conference calls. You should write down your tasks in tickets, hold a quick stand-up meeting, and maybe keep a chat thread running. If you start setting up conference calls, your people will be bored, and you might get sucked into a time sink. I have never heard someone say "I worked on this project with a lot of conference calls, and it went great!" This never happens. Prove me wrong, I dare you.

It's nice to do a big kickoff call to make sure everyone on the team has heard your plan. After that, when you do group calls, include only the right people. Choose carefully. Your listeners will appreciate the call if it is actually relevant for them.

Job interviews

It takes a long time set up job interviews, and more time to do them. If you go straight from a resume to a paid trial task, you get to the work more quickly. You might also get better results. Job interviews are deceptive. You might think you are hiring someone because they proved they can do a good job, but statistically, about half of the time they are just good at interviews, or they matched some preconceived notion that you had about how a good job candidate should look. That's why orchestras often hold auditions behind a screen. Try trials.

Estimates

A lot of technology, skill, and time goes into estimating how long things will take. In many cases this expenditure of time and treasure is useless. Often you can skip the estimates and get your real work done faster, or take the time that you save and do something equally useless on Facebook or Twitter.

Let's look at situations where time estimates are useless:

- You already know the order in which you are going to work on tasks, and no estimate is going to change that. This is the big time-saver. There is no reason to spend time on an activity that never changes your outputs. If you can put tasks into priority order with a good roadmap, you will not need to estimate.

- You already know how much time and money you are willing to spend on the project. This is the typical reality. Regardless of your estimate, the project is worth a certain amount of time and money. As an entrepreneur, I recommend this time-boxing, money-boxing approach. Given a new product idea, I am perfectly happy to say that it should take X weeks to build and not more. A bigger organization might pretend that they care about how long you think it SHOULD take, but most of the time they are lying to make you feel better. Or they are self-delusional. You can deal with this by using the Agile method of prioritizing, and always having a release that you can ship, however partially complete.

- The estimate is going to be wrong anyway. There are ways to improve estimates (reduction to detail, self-estimates, historical velocity, etc.). However, some projects have a lot of dependencies and uncertainties, and over a certain size of project estimates are almost always wrong. You can use the tactic of tracking your estimates and comparing them to actual velocity. If estimates get better with this technique, then keep doing them. If they keep going off track, then maybe it's best to give up and work on prioritizing better.

Task scheduling

Task scheduling is an even bigger waste of time than estimating. You can learn to estimate correctly, but you never do tasks in the order of the original schedule. Then you end up spending more time adjusting the schedule to match reality. That is why we schedule by stacking a bunch of tasks (not ordered or scheduled) to be done before a milestone date. You can do them in any order, and you don't have to spend time fixing the schedule.

Fixed specifications

It always takes longer to do work with a fixed scope or fixed specification. You have to gather requirements, make the specification, do some difficult estimating, and agree on the business deal, BEFORE YOU CAN START. In the same amount of time a team that had simply started and worked incrementally might have finished something better than your original spec.

You may feel like a winner when you purchase services using a fixed specification, but if gathering information and creating the spec take longer than performing the services, you come out behind. You can get good results from an Agile team by starting quickly and setting a fixed price for a fixed time.

Dividing work geographically

It might seem like a nice simplification of roles, to send your requirements to Chicago, your coding to Bangalore, and your testing to Lima. I think this wastes talent and makes your life harder. Why not hire people in all of your locations that can handle the complete process?

Anything important on Post-it notes

Post-it notes have a glamorous role in the world of Agile Scrum and
Kanban teams. They represent the power and intimacy of small team.
Using Post-it notes, you throw out ideas with a satisfying squelch. You
rearrange and reorganize your task board on a whim.

But Post-it notes also cause problems. They are bad for distributed team
members, or even for someone who happens to be home with a sick
child. If someone is not in the room, handling the paper, they aren't
included at all. There is only one version of posted truth, and alternative
organizations are not considered. Worst of all, at the end of an iteration
you throw away all the information on the notes.

Post-it notes are an instrument of oppression and control. You use them
to control access to the task board. You use them to oppress anyone who
is not in the room with you. You use them to erase institutional memory
and rewrite the past. You can chew them up and eat the evidence.

In a world with lots of good online ticketing and issue management
systems, there's no excuse for the tyranny of Post-it notes. You should
put your notes and task boards online where everyone can comment, and
you don't lose the information.

High-Performing Teams

A popular theory holds that team members need to get to know each other socially through "Forming, Storming and Norming" before they can get to "Performing." You can blame this theory for a lot of silly team building exercises. It leads people to believe that they need to have an expensive and delay-inducing meeting before their distributed team can start performing.

Fortunately, an observation of high-performing teams shows that this theory is backward. Actually, people like to join teams where they can get to work and achieve a goal. Later, after they see they have been "performing," they start to feel very warmly toward their fellow teammates. According to team expert and Harvard professor J. Richard Hackman: "The cause-and-effect is the reverse of what most people believe: When we're productive and we've done something good together we feel satisfied, not the other way around."

Why is it better to start with performing and get to bonding later? Because people want to do a good job. They spend a lot of time at work, and they don't want to waste that time. They don't actually need peer pressure to want to do a good job.

Your distributed team can be a high-performing team even if they never socialize together. Socializing is nice, but it's nice because it makes people feel good, not because it makes them more productive.

Wisdom of teams

In the book "Wisdom of Teams," McKinsey consultants Smith and Katzenberg observed that:

- High performing teams always have a shared goal. They organize around the shared goal.

- Teams can be high performing even if they don't meet and work together, and even when they don't like each other. Smith and Katzenberg found that this was true even in the 1980s when remote workers were connected only by big, heavy telephones. And Hackman says that teams will perform better if they have a "deviant" - the annoying guy who brings up opposing viewpoints.

- "Team" organizations have rotating leadership. For example, a software team might find that a designer is leading at the beginning, while a programmer with architecture skills steps forward to get past a difficult technical hurdle, and a DevOps person takes charge to get everyone working toward reliable deployments.

- "Single-leader" organizations have one person who tells everyone else what to do. Single leader organization work great when the leader knows exactly what to do. But team organizations adapt to change, which is a key objective of Agile projects. If you value the team organization, you will let people step forward from any location, rather than assigning roles by location.

So successful groups start with a goal, make progress toward the goal, then bond into a team. You can help your distributed teams follow these steps.

If you have a lot of opinion-based arguments, political lobbying and factions, you probably lack a strong shared goal. Politics emerges in the absence of the pressure of a shared goal. When people come under pressure to achieve clear goals they become more focused on facts and will agree more.

Shared values?

It is nice if your team shares some values about collaboration and productivity. However, sharing isn't essential, and it can come later in the process. You do not need to force people into a group value system. During World War II the Americans and Soviets didn't share many political values, but because they shared a goal they teamed up into a mighty fighting force. The people that make an iPhone make a beautiful product efficiently. They live in the US, Japan, China, and many other countries. They live in mansions, boats, and dormitories. Do they share values? I doubt it. They don't have to. They share a supply chain.

Productivity comes from shared GOALS, not shared values, and from a process that is structured to allow people to do their jobs separately yet work together. As long as they share a goal and have room to work, they can ignore each other's values. If you are going to insist on shared values, you are going to have a very short supply chain - probably just 5 or 10 people sitting around a campfire singing Kumbaya. That sounds like a Scrum team! Make people more productive, and you can go global.

Retrospectives and happiness surveys

To start the cycle of success, you will need something like a supply chain. You will need a process that works to deliver a great product. How do you get a process that works? Get feedback from your team members.

In traditional Scrum, you do a "retrospective" after each sprint where the team talks about what went right, what went wrong, and what should be done differently in the next sprint. This is a powerful tool for improving your process and making sure that it constantly adapts.

However, it can also be tedious work.

A "happiness survey" is a similar idea that can be applied to more cases (including continuous delivery) and that requires less meeting time. I got the idea from Henrik Kniberg and Jeff Sutherland. A happiness survey only takes a few minutes to fill out, so you can do it during any cycle. It uncovers a broad range of improvement opportunities.

A happiness survey can be conducted through an online form or spreadsheet (e.g. a Google spreadsheet) with the following fields:

- Name

- Happiness Rating (1-5)

- "What feels best right now?"

- "What feels worst right now?"

- "What would increase your happiness?"

- Other Comments

After you conduct a happiness survey you will be under pressure to act on the results. If you don't act, people will see the survey as a waste of time and your happiness initiatives will die an unhappy death.

There is also a risk that people will write complaints of the "life sucks and then you die" variety. You can't prevent that. However, I am usually very happy with the results of this type of survey. People write in about specific problems, with actionable suggestions. Most of the time they suggest ways to improve productivity. This goes to prove that people are highly motivated to do a good job.

I like the happiness survey better than a traditional retrospective for two reasons:

1. Traditional retrospectives have a tendency to drone on, become boring, and end without reaching conclusions. A happiness survey is more bounded. The team and team leaders only need to address issues that were mentioned in the survey.

2. Traditional retrospectives are dominated by the most vocal members of the team. These are not always the most careful observers. With a happiness survey everyone can make an equal contribution, and some of the less vocal team members contribute good points.

Private language

One sign that you have a high-performing team is that they develop their own language. I worked on a team that built around a source code system called SourceSafe, which they called "SourceCow" for its plodding ways, and then just "the Cow." Pretty soon everything was named as some sort of cow. Those guys herded a lot of cows very effectively. So it is a good sign if you drop in on a team and can't understand what they are saying.

Crossing cultures

I often get asked if my team suffers from problems in communication caused by cultural differences. For instance, "Yes I can do it" might mean different things to people from different countries. However, I rarely if ever see that problem. All of the members of my team are culturally similar. They are geeks. They are engineers. They focus on facts and they quickly decide what they think is achievable or not achievable. They may feel awkward in their home countries, but they are at home on our team. They have a nature that is more powerful than their nurture. If you think a shared culture is important, then your recruiting process - how you select people - will be more important than the locations that you recruit in.

Tech Leads

If you have a fast, continuous, distributed team, you will do a lot of communicating around code: code review and code releases. You will get less use from non-technical project managers, because they don't communicate in code. You need "Technical Leads" - programmers who can communicate in code and lead a small team.

At a Google office the other day, I heard someone say "Tech Leads make all the decisions at Google." They also make the decisions here at Assembla. If you do continuous Agile development, they will make decisions in your organization.

A Tech Lead or Technical Lead is a software engineer who also leads a small programming team. Tech Lead should be able to:

- Work closely with product managers and story owners to design features and prioritize tasks.

- Support teams by answering questions and solving problems.

- Assemble releases and drive improvements in release processes.

- Help with recruiting and hiring.

- And – write code.

Why is understanding code a requirement for people who lead development teams? Because teams and contributors are far more efficient when they communicate with code instead of words, especially when contributors are distributed. Because someone who understands code is better able to support teams and manage releases. And because software engineers respect people who can code.

What about Scrum Masters – aren't they an essential part of Agile? I say no, not at all. You may want to employ a consultant with skills in coaching and "removing impediments." But they can't take the responsibility to delivery your product. A tech lead will.

Can engineers manage?

Tech Lead is a tough job, and some say that engineers can't do it. You might have heard people say "a good engineer is a bad manager." I don't believe it. There was a time when people said that engineers made bad entrepreneurs. Today, software engineers run the most successful technology companies, and the hottest startups.

Our campaign to help hackers build tech lead skills is similar to the campaign that Paul Graham has waged at YCombinator to teach hackers how to be good entrepreneurs. The end result will eventually be successful technical CEO's like Bill Gates and Eric Schmidt.

However, if you have tried to hire leaders for your technical teams, you know that it is hard to get good people. Our goal is to make it easier to train tech leads, by teaching a minimum set of skills that will get a good programmer started as a tech lead.

We think that good developers can become good Tech Leads by practicing a small set of new skills and responsibilities.

The Tech Lead Checklist

We have developed a checklist of daily, weekly and bi-weekly tasks to help our Tech Leads plan their major activities. Here it is:

DAILY

- Require written standup reports each day. Read ALL standup reports. If someone did not write a standup report, contact them by chat or email, and escalate if they do not respond.

- Attend a daily chat based on the standup reports. Ask for comments and issues. Make it short. Move long discussions offline.

- Resolve needs and roadblocks posted in the standup reports and raised in the daily chat.

- Look at the detailed activity report for each developer.

- Document requests and agreements on a ticket, in a message, or on a wiki. Do not rely on verbal agreements, because they can't be tracked.

- Let team members select their own tasks. Balance the load. Do not let team members work on many tickets concurrently. A team member should select one or two tickets to work on and finish. The rest are available for others to select.

- If someone has been working for several days on one ticket without committing code, ask him or her to split the ticket into smaller tasks.

WEEKLY

- Review all tickets currently in process (for Kanban or Lean processes), or in the current iteration or milestone (for Scrum or Scrumban processes). Add or move tickets depending on schedule and capacity.

- Ask specific developers to take the planning and task breakdown for complex tickets, features, stories. To distribute the load, obtain mockups and stories from non-developer product owners.

- Write and post a message about what the team did last week and what the team will do next week.

BI-WEEKLY TEAM BUILDING

- Work with your recruiters to help them locate people with the right skills for the team (but let them handle the details of finding candidates).

- Do "onboarding." Make sure every new developer has the information he or she needs, a development environment, and a simple task. Update setup documentation that outlines team processes such as the standup reports, the daily chat, the task planning process and the code management workflow.

- Evaluate trial developers near the end of the trial period. Assess their productivity and quality. Write a short review. Say whether you want to continue working with them.

Some traditional Scrum Masters will say the Tech Lead process described here is micro-management, and that it is better to set weekly goals and let the team work out its own schedule. I love you guys, and we should get together for a big, warm group hug. But we should do it AFTER we use these tactics to build a highly productive team that feels great because they are doing kickass coding.

Job satisfaction

Developing the Tech Lead role improves everyone's morale.

Developers interested in career development like the Tech Lead role because they get to take on more responsibilities, develop management skills, and progress in their careers.

Developers who don't want to become managers still like having managers who are technical.

Business managers love working with development staff who understand both business priorities and technical issues and have a realistic view of schedules and deliverables.

Development executives find that Tech Leads allow them to utilize more distributed teams, more efficient workflows, and better development talent.

Outsourcers

"Our people are just as bad as your people, and cheaper"

Companies that outsource IT operations are often very successful. How do they succeed? I think that they often replace in-house IT staff with operational roles rather than those doing product development work. The managers in their client companies are often unhappy with their own IT staff. The outsourcers essentially promise "Our people are just as bad as your people, and cheaper." Their cheaper model works well for many IT tasks. It is not working well for product development.

We have seen particular problems with Indian outsourcing firms. We went through a phase where we took candidates from outsourcing firms and worked with them on two-week trial contracts. The salespeople from these firms promised, over and over again, that we were getting their best programming talent. However, the results were disappointing. About 10% of these candidates performed at an acceptable level. When we select our own individual contributors for trials we have a success rate of around 50%. These results explain why Silicon Valley firms often pay more than $100 per hour for local talent, even though Indian outsourcers offer similar services for $20 per hour.

There are many talented individual contractors working on the Internet, from many countries. The Assembla team currently includes 43 people from 16 countries. There are also (in theory) many talented people working in outsourcing firms. These companies promise professional management in addition to programming talent. Some of these outsourcers are good. However, in our experience, outsourcing firms are often useless for software product development. You can protect yourself if you understand their incentives, and take some of the actions recommended below, such as moving to fully transparent continuous agile.

We can see how the incentives of Indian outsourcing vendors work against product development projects:

- They want to get big customers and big jobs. Big customers are much more profitable than small customers. This fact explains most of the problems that a small customer will have in getting good talent. The outsourcers have a limited supply of top talent, and they make it available to their biggest customers, but not their small customers.

- They often get paid by the hour, so they give you the cheapest person that matches your buzzword. They get no benefit from productivity improvements. In fact, they get paid more if jobs take longer.

- They have high turnover. Turnover at an outsourcing firm is often high. It's even higher for the best people, because they get poached. It's much higher for the customers that are working with the best people, because those people often get pulled off onto bigger or newer clients. Outsourcing firms double the natural turnover by pulling people off projects. Also, outsourcing firms cover up turnover by hiding their individual contributors behind project managers. This is inefficient.

Protect yourself

Here are some strategies for protecting yourself when working with outsourcing companies:

- Insist on individual accountability. You should have individual logins, code commits, standup reports, and activity streams from every contributor. This will help you find the good contributors, address problems quickly, and react to turnover. It also gives you a good, friendly working environment.

- Be the biggest customer (or buy the firm). If you are the biggest customer, you will get the best talent. Most big technology companies eventually figure this out and ensure that they get the best talent by buying their outsourcing suppliers and becoming the only customer.

- Build around tech leads. If you can't buy an outsourcing company, you can probably buy a good tech lead. Remote tech leads will often offer to find a team of like-minded individuals to work with them.

- Learn to manage a distributed, global team. You may feel dependent on the outsourcing model, where you get a remote office that you can manage with your co-located management skills. However, that model gives you limited access to the best talent. If you learn to manage a truly distributed global team, you will be able to work with the very best contractors and outsourcers.

Find the right outsourcer

There are attributes you can look for to find an outsourcer that can do real software engineering and development. It might be the beginning of a beautiful friendship.

Specialization. A lot of outsourcing companies claim to do almost everything. That is a bad sign. They may have one person in the company who has done each thing they claim to know. That doesn't mean that the team assigned to you will have any relevant experience. It is a good sign when the whole company is specialized. They are probably very good at their specialty.

Fixed price options. Offering a fixed price option shows that the firm has confidence in its ability to manage and deliver. I don't usually recommend buying development services for a fixed price because it causes delays. You need extra time to specify and negotiate work and to test and accept the deliverable. However, I think it is a good sign if the firm offers a fixed price option, and a good idea to test it.

Practicing continuous delivery. This gives you a lot of visibility into the development process, and creates many places where you can work together for improvement. Use a continuous agile process to get individual accountability, engagement, and a good workflow for distributed team members.

Recruiting and Team Building

The most important contributor to success in any project is the talent and commitment of the people working on it. Good people do the right thing, do it fast, and do it with minimal intervention. This is especially true in software development, where the good engineers are anecdotally reported to be ten times as productive as the average contributor. If you believe this (I believe it), you will invest heavily in getting and keeping the right people.

 Managing a distributed team is not easy. If you are doing the work, you should insist on getting the benefit. The benefit is that you can work with good people, even if they cannot come to your office. If you are having trouble getting the right people into your office, you can expand with a distributed team.

Here are some hints from on our own experience building distributed teams.

Trials

We hire people that we have never met. Instead of interviews, we do trials. If we like someone on paper, we offer them a temporary contract, usually two weeks. Then, we ask them to help us with some real work. Usually, we can see if we want to work together within the first few days. At the end of the trial period, if we like the candidate, and the candidate likes us, we try to set up long-term job agreement.

Trials are often faster than doing interviews. We find that it often takes two weeks find the right people to talk to the candidate, schedule times, and get feedback. If you measure this in your own organization, you will be surprised at how long it takes. And, the time that you spend on interviews costs you money. Trials can be cheaper, even if you pay the candidate well.

Trials can also improve results. I have found that when I hire people for on-site work, even after doing careful interviews, there is only about a 50% probability that the person will stay long term. Half the time, they have a problem with us, or we have a problem with them, and they leave within 3 months. This finding is consistent across many different companies and job types. It is disruptive and expensive for both sides.

There is some evidence that trials give better results if you do not meet the candidates. When you interview someone, you won't select the person who does the best work. You will select the person that you like. In the book "Blink", Malcolm Gladwell tells the story of orchestra recruiters who compared a process with a personal interview, and an audition, with a process where they listened to candidates play an audition piece from behind a screen. It turns out that personal interviews tended to result in the hiring affable, good looking men. Without the screen, the personal, visual impression of the candidate is so powerful that it actually affects the sound that the committee heard. They thought they were selecting the best audition player, but when they used the screen, and really were able to listen to the audition, they heard differently. The human mind, your mind and mine, is filled with powerful biases. Some of those biases are useful for making quick decisions, and some are just misleading. You can use trials to make sure that candidates are good at the work.

Succeeding with trials

Over many years, we have discovered things that help us succeed with trials.

Use a standard contract and contracting process. We built an entire oDesk style contracting system into Assembla to manage these contracts and payments. It's worth it. You can set up an internal process to bring in candidates, or use a crowdsourcing site.

Make sure the candidate is really available. The most common cause of failure in trials is that the candidate does not show up for work. If the candidate has a different job, they will almost always overestimate the free time they have available. Get a full time commitment, or assume a part-time commitment will only be 10 hours per week.

Don't let an outsourcing project manager or recruiter obscure the identity of the candidates. You want individual talent and commitment.

Do real work. You can give people a test task. This helps you compare one candidate to another. However, I think this gives you a lower probability of succeeding with the trial. The candidate will see that it is just a test task. The internal leader that is running the trial will not spend much effort to help the candidate do a good job, because he doesn't need the work. It's just a test. If both sides are working on a real task that the project needs, they will pay more attention. The trial will succeed more often.

Save beginner tasks. You should keep a list of tasks that you can give to candidates.

Provide a lot of support in the early stages. You will get good results if the candidate feels like part of the team from the first day. Sometimes, the trial leader will spend time with candidates. If the trial leaders are busy, you can ask a team member or admin person to communicate with the candidate every day for the first few days.

Do a formal evaluation at the scheduled end of the trial. It is easy to let this task be delayed if you have a lot of work. However, it will hurt your recruiting, and recruiting is the most important thing that you do. I recommend asking an administrative person to send out "What did you think / What did you accomplish" messages. Send them to both the candidate, and the trial leader. Do this promptly just before the end of the trial.

Recruiting: Go outside, go global.

A lot of people do recruiting by asking friends, relatives, business acquaintances, and employees for referrals. If your referrers are enthusiastic supporters, they can persuade some great people to become candidates. That's a terrific result. However you should not depend on this strategy because it is statistically a bad bet. I call it the "ask your cousin" strategy. Would you rather select from 50 people that your cousin knows, or 5000 people reading an advertisement? Even if you are getting a good flow of referrals, look at outside candidates to make sure that the referral process is giving you better candidates.

Write the job description and post it. The act of writing a job description and agreeing on it will get your own team involved, and make the recruiting more likely to succeed. Posting it will get you candidates.

Post as widely as possible. Use both general and specialized online job boards. Use internal forums to post jobs inside big companies.

If you are assembling a new team from employees of a big company, you can still use these tactics. You can write and post team openings on internal communication boards. You can insist on a trial period, and on the ability to select the people you want.

Crowdsourcing sites are good sources of leads. They fit naturally with a trial process. Read the terms of the crowdsourcing agreement carefully. Look for agreements that allow you to work more directly with a "provider" when you find a good one.

Tech Leads

You will need an internal team leader to work with your trial candidates. You should train people for this role. To work with programming candidates, you will need a Tech Lead. Please see our "Tech Lead Checklist" for a description of Tech Lead tasks, including recruiting and team onboarding.

Equal opportunity

I like working with truly global teams where a person in any location can grow to do any job. Try to remove obstacles based on location, contracts, or history

Full-time attention

You will get best results if you can get full-time attention from your team members. When possible, try to organize full time jobs, and not part time jobs.

Getting attention can be a problem in "functional" organizations. You may only get a small slice of an expert's time. According to lean theory, you will get good results if the functional experts focus full time on one task until they finish it, even if they have a lot of tasks waiting. You can help functional experts by setting up a Kanban board where they can display the work that is waiting, and show the WIP. They will appreciate the opportunity to finish their WIP.

Long-term retention

If your project is complicated, you want to keep people long term. It takes a long time to build knowledge of a complicated system, and you want to keep the people that have that knowledge. Here are some things to think about:

- Insulation. Does the team member work directly for you? Can you personally address their concerns and professional goals?

- Competition from other projects. This can be especially severe if you are working in a big company, or working with outsourcers.

- Advancement: How does this project meet their professional goals for the next year?

- Rotation. Retention has its downside. People will get tired of a project. You need a way to rotate them to fresh challenges, permanently or temporarily.

Scaling

The Most Expensive Problem in Tech

In 1965, IBM released the System 360 with its associated operating system, OS/360. This was the largest computer development project ever attempted, and it cost $5B, equivalent to $38B in 2013. IBM was almost broken by this huge expenditure, and by delays in delivering OS/360. However, they persevered and they won the prize, becoming the largest, most profitable, and most powerful corporation on earth as the System 360 grabbed a monopoly position in datacenters across the world.

The leader of the OS/360 project, Fred Brooks, came under incredible pressure. He observed that in complex software projects the productivity of individual developers degrades to the point where "adding manpower to a late software project makes it later." He wrote a book analyzing the problem called "The Mythical Man Month," and eventually retired to academia.

Fifty years later, the same problems are with us, and we still read the Mythical Man Month. It's still true that big software projects are the most expensive and dangerous investments in the high-tech business. More than half of large projects never finish. Some of these are the $100M government agency disasters that you hear about on the news, and some of them are private problems that show up in bankruptcy court.

Big projects are a huge drain on individual productivity. The statistics in Software Assessments, Benchmarks and Best Practices put numbers to the scaling effect. Productivity is measured at 15 function points per developer month for software having 100 function points, declining to 5 per developer month for projects having 10,000 function points, at which point 67 people were involved. The author notes that "projects having more than 100,000 function points are more likely to fail than to succeed." Typical staff size on these projects was 690. There lie dragons.

Scaling problems also afflict small projects. For example, when you go from 1 person to 2 people, you get a big decline in developer productivity. I usually estimate that you need two developers working 40 hours per week to replace one developer working 60 hours per week. That is exactly why good developers work such long hours. Improved scaling ratios will have a disproportionate benefit for small teams that need vacations.

A modern solution to the problem is to shrink the size of programming teams. We improve the productivity of individual developers by giving them better tools, better programming environments, and more shared open source code. Because each developer is more productive, you can build the same software with a smaller team. Working in a smaller team adds additional productivity. So, the multiplier effect works in reverse, and a team of 10 can do what a team of 100 did in years past.

Another modern solution to the problem is to eliminate big projects by chopping them up into smaller services. We will explore this tactic later.

However, eventually those services get integrated into a big system. Some projects are just big. Intelligent systems with big data are big. Data and phone networks are big. Like IBM, the platform providers that can build and manage these big systems will win big prizes.

Fortunately, we have new tactics for managing these projects that have evolved as the Internet has grown. Brooks warned us that there is no silver bullet that can kill the beasts that afflict large projects. However, the following pages will present a bag of silver shrapnel.

This chapter is under construction. We will soon post new content here on subjects like:

- Scalable Agile

- Eliminating batches and meetings

- Dependencies - and how to vanquish the Mythical Man Month

- Service architecture

Scalable Agile Flow

The Scalable Agile process is a way to manage a big project with a big group of contributors. It is designed to include teams and contributors even if they do not have the same organization and cycle (for example, they are not all Scrum teams with the same two-week schedule). As your projects get bigger, they will come to resemble the diagram below.

1) You prioritize the work in a sorted backlog. To make this more scalable, you can use the "Epics and Allocations" technique to include multiple planners and programs.

2) Your contributors go to work. They can use their own team management methods (including Scrum). There are no fixed resource constraints. New contributors can join and take tasks.

3) Contributors get their own test environments. They use a distributed continuous delivery process to test and submit changes.

4) You assemble a release by taking the contributions that are ready and meet all of your standards. You can release at any time, or continuously. You can precisely control contributors, quality, and standards.by deciding what to take.

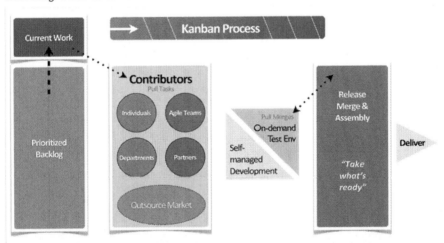

Why does this work?

You are in many cases managing code, rather than people. Code can be precisely managed and controlled, accepted or rejected. People are very difficult to manage and impossible to control. It's much easier to focus on motivating them.

There is less planning. There is no iteration plan. You plan at the end with a "take what's ready" approach. Instead of planning, you prioritize, which is easier.

There are several powerful control points. You control the backlog. You control the allocation of tasks to contributors by approving, rejecting, or setting time and budget limits. You control the code and changes that you accept into the final release. This gives you a much more effective way to enforce code, test, and architecture standards, compared to an approach which relies on policy and education.

Advantages

- Fast. Release when ready. Take the right duration, long or short

- Distributed and Dispersed teams. No big meetings or requirement for mass consensus

- Scales to more contributors. No centralized iteration planning or testing. Include new contributors and many types of contributors

- Scrum compatible. If you have productive Scrum teams, they can work as contributors with zero process change.

Meetings

When you start work on a big project, you may get a sinking feeling as you think "big meetings." Team members don't like meetings because they are boring. Project managers don't like meetings because they take time to arrange, which can substantially delay projects. Businesses don't like meetings because they are very expensive in time and money.

But we still call meetings. They are efficient for managers, who only have to explain themselves once, rather than many times in many media. They also provide a place for team members to ask questions and get help.

When we go continuous and get rid of batches, like iterations and releases, we Unblock! and become more scalable. Meetings are also batches, and they block. Our teams will be more scalable if we reduce the number of meetings.

Let's look at some of the most common types of meetings and see how we can eliminate them or get more out of them.

Kickoff

A face-to-face kickoff meeting at the beginning of a project gives you a chance to present the big vision and goals of the project and answer questions. This is one of the most productive types of meetings, because it aligns everyone with the same goals. That makes your teams more effective. It is also a chance to answer questions from skeptics. You hope that it will launch contributors into productive work quickly.

However, the kickoff meeting comes at an inconvenient time, just when you want to get started quickly. If it takes time to bring people together for this meeting, you should not accept the delay.

You can do an online presentation that will be almost as effective. Present the vision, goals, plan and roles of the project, then take questions. Do not try to turn this event into a working and planning session. Your teams will do that later, after you have inspired them. Make the presentation, answer questions, then finish.

Make architecture proposals and prototypes before you do a kickoff meeting. Architecture is a solitary art, not a group sport. Your champions should bring solid proposals into any kickoff.

Daily standup

Your team can post "What I did," "What I will do today" and "What I need" on an online form. That saves a lot of time. After that they can hold an online chat and discuss needs and questions. As your team becomes more confident, they may eliminate the scheduled chat and just use persistent chat to post questions and victories as events occur.

I recommend that you keep the "what I will do today" reporting because it gives you a chance to see when people are working on low priority tasks and ask them to help with high priority tasks.

Client reports

If you provide development services to clients, you probably do a weekly call with each client to show your work and report on how things are going. You will want to make this easier and more professional with a fixed format agenda, similar to the standup format. It is very important to include "what I need from the client" in this agenda. In a continuous process, your goal should be to shrink the number of people on this call to a very small number, such as two. To do this, you should provide ways for clients and service teams to communicate directly, in real time.

Iteration plan

I recommend that you eliminate iteration planning meetings. They are a lot of work, and they are difficult for a distributed team. Instead, use a process like Scrumban or Kanban that allows users to pull tasks when they are ready to work on them.

Instead of doing an iteration plan with the complete team, take a smaller group of people and do "backlog grooming." This means making sure that your upcoming tasks have good descriptions, use cases, and design materials. Ask if they are still urgent and important. Present your implementation team with tasks that are worth doing, and the information they need for success.

Ad hoc

You should arrange meetings to brainstorm and resolve problems, if they become urgent. These meetings are good because they bring together a selected group of people who are actually interested in the issue. One secret to getting enthusiastic participation is to not make meetings all about you. Make sure that a substantial proportion of the meetings are called for other people's problems. You should also show that the meetings are meaningful by following up on any recommendations coming from them.

Retrospective

If continuous improvement is a core goal, retrospective meetings are an important tool to figure out how to improve. However, for some reason most retrospectives are incredibly boring. Consider these alternatives:

- Make improvement a continuous process that fits into planning and all other tasks.

- To get team input, try a happiness survey. It tends to focus attention on a smaller set of issues, and it gives everyone a voice. After you do the survey, make a list of issues, present them in a chat, and collect ideas for improvement.

Scrum of Scrums

These big cross-team meetings are a major weak point in applying Scrum to larger projects. They are useful (when they work) because they give people a chance to handle dependencies. If one team is waiting for something from a second team, they can ask for help and get a status update at the Scrum of Scrums level. But there are better ways to handle dependencies, which we will discuss in the next section.

Dependencies

It's very important to manage dependencies in a large project, because the whole project will grind to a halt if too many people are waiting for (are dependent on) other people's output.

There are three ways to manage dependencies. If you run a big project, you will need to keep ALL of these mechanisms working efficiently. Projects fail when any one of these mechanisms gets jammed. Projects scale when they all work well.

1) Top-down planning

A manager must make a plan to ensure that certain tasks are finished first. This is always required for the big stuff. If you want a carpenter to come to frame a house, you need a plan to make sure that someone pours the foundation first. You can't expect the carpenter to arrange that after he shows up.

However, a project planner can't know everything. The team will need to figure out a lot of the plan and the dependencies while working. That is why we need peer-to-peer communication.

2) Peer-to-peer communication

In a smoothly-running project people and teams figure out what they depend on (what they are waiting for) and communicate with the people who can give them what they need. This is particularly important for projects facing unknowns, like those involving innovation or working with variable scope.

There are three major types of communication:

- **Peer-to-peer communication.** Each individual contacts the person whose output is needed. This is the most efficient method of communication.

- **The big meeting.** Everyone participates in a meeting, presents outputs they are waiting for, and gets help. This is the theory behind "Scrum of Scrums" meetings

- **Escalation to management.** People escalate dependencies to managers, who seek help from other parts of the organization. This might be necessary because people are not responding to peer-to-peer requests, or because nobody has been assigned to produce a needed deliverable. People can escalate needs with a message to their manager, or by raising an "obstacle" in a standup. Also, managers can run reports that show tasks that are likely to be blocked, and act on those.

We can make escalation easier by showing the problems that need to be escalated on a report. For example, it is possible to add a "relation" on ticket B that says it is waiting for ticket A, then run a report showing who is waiting for tasks that are unassigned or abandoned.

3) Fix it yourself

If something is important, you can fix it yourself, rather than waiting for someone else to do it.

The importance of this escape valve should not be underestimated. I think that it accounts for all of the improvement in scalability that open source projects experience over commercial projects. If you share code and responsibility, people can eliminate their own obstacles.

Most projects use a combination of these techniques. Big projects always require a project plan. New activities require communication. Important and easy tasks will yield to fix-it-yourself.

Do we need the Scrum of Scrums meetings? In my opinion, meetings are **not** required. We can handle everything that was not in the high-level project plan with peer-to-peer communication, organizational escalation, and the fix-it-yourself escape valve.

Mythical Man Month, Revisited

The Mythical Man Month is a classic book from Frederick Brooks that considers the problem of large software projects which tend to move slowly and have low productivity. There are two frustrating aspects to this. The first frustrating aspect is that everyone gets slowed down. A programmer who can produce 100 debugged lines per day on a small project might only manage 10 on a big project. The second frustrating aspect is that it seems impossible to speed up by adding labor. Brooks noted that "Adding manpower to a late software project makes it later" (Brook's Law). He also pointed out that "Nine women can't make a baby in one month."

Brooks hypothesizes that this problem stems from a sort of communication overload. If N people are working on a project they have N^2 ways to talk to each other. That gets to be a lot of work as N increases. He then suggests some ways to reduce communication load through specialization (for example, a tool master) and modularization, breaking the project into functional groups that only communicate inside a small part of the hierarchy.

It's clear that big projects are slow, hard to manage and hard to accelerate. However, I am not persuaded by Brooks' analysis of the problem. There are 6 billion people in the world but I don't have to send them all a Christmas card or write on their Facebook walls. Nobody forces you to communicate with them.

I propose an alternate hypothesis based on dependencies. One person cannot be slowed down waiting for himself. In a big project, a lot people are waiting for components from other people. If 100 people are working and 50 people are waiting for something, then you are already down to 50% of potential productivity. The problem could actually become a lot worse if everyone is waiting for a few critical components.

We could model a project mathematically as an "NK network" where N people are each dependent on K components in active development. The behavior of this type of model is sensitive to K but not very sensitive to increases in N. In our example it would be sensitive to dependencies rather than the number of people. NK networks don't behave smoothly. They have a tendency to "phase shift," or lock up suddenly. After the lockup most people would be waiting for something. Maybe that is one reason that continuous delivery teams can scale to a large size. The continuous delivery system is tuned to detect and fix lockups.

Communication versus dependency

The two theories both agree that you should maximize the amount of encapsulation - libraries and services - to keep most communication and dependencies inside one team.

From there the two theories lead you in different directions. If you believe that you have a communication problem, then you want to minimize the amount of communication. If you believe that you have a dependency problem, then you believe that more communication is better because it helps people work around the obstacles.

Fortunately, we have broken through the Brooks Barrier and we can see how. We use transparency and sharing. For example, the Linux kernel has grown by a steady 10% per year even as the number of contributors has increased to more than 1000. In the dependency theory, open source projects have a scaling advantage because all code is shared. If someone is waiting for a component and they are frustrated enough and talented enough, they can just fix the problem. The open source answer to the dependency problem is more communication and more potential overlap.

Internet projects tend to communicate in writing on tickets, blogs, mailing lists and wikis that are accessible to all team members. This changes the communication from a network of conversations that take time from a lot of people to a simple text search that a team member can do individually. It collapses the N^2 network. Perhaps this is why the time spent on conference calls, which do fit in the N^2 network, is a good indicator of management problems.

Escaping Brooks' Law

You can escape Brooks' Law if you are only adding people, and not dependencies between people. This could happen in theory if you had a centrally planned set of services with perfect encapsulation. There are a couple of other cases where you can escape, and you should try these if you are under a lot of time pressure.

Pile on at the beginning. You can add a large number of people at the beginning of a project. At the very beginning of a project, nobody knows what they are doing. It doesn't drag down the average expertise to add more people. In most projects, the number of contributors starts small and increases through the first big post-beta release. If you are under a lot of time pressure, you can put in a bulge of people at the beginning. Then, you weed out the ineffective contributors, and you even take some good people away to trim down the team size. Now, you have a hidden advantage, because you can bring those people back as the project ramps up, and they will understand the project. I do this, and it works.

Do it twice. You can run two completely separate efforts to solve a problem, and then take the solution that arrives first, or the one that gives you the best result. You don't have any scaling problems because the projects are completely separate. This is a common way to handle architecture questions. You ask two people to try two different approaches, and you take the one you like best. It's also what you do when failure is not an option. When the United States was racing against Germany to build an atom bomb, they funded three different uranium enrichment tactics and two different bomb designs.

Engineers hate having two people or teams assigned to the same task. It seems inefficient and it really bothers them. However, business people should love this idea. It's a lot cheaper to pay two people to fix something fast, than it is to pay 100 people to wait around for one person to do it more slowly.

Service Architecture

Service architecture is the secret weapon that the big Silicon Valley firms are using to scale both systems, and teams.

Small projects are more efficient and easier to manage than big projects. We can make big software smaller by chopping it into pieces called "services." Services are separate processes, programs, servers, or business processes that have a defined interface. You can write tests to make sure that services respond the way you expect. As a system grows it will inevitably be divided into services.

Services are everywhere already

Services are everywhere. If you make a Web application or Web site, you are providing services to a browser. And, you already have all of the problems with versioning services, because you are serving multiple types and versions of browsers. If you make mobile apps you are providing services to the mobile client. Installed software calls operating system services. Datacenter software calls database servers and storage and many other services.

Separate services make it easy to release frequently

It's difficult to release a big system reliably, with reversibility and low risk. It's much easier if you are releasing a smaller component or service. You can streamline the process of deploying it (or rolling back). You can rely on automated tests to qualify the service for release, because it has a defined interface that you can test.

Here are some strategies to get started with services that you can release more frequently or continuously:

1) Wrap old code into services. Define an API or an interface to the old software, and write automated tests to make sure that it works the way you expect.

2) Put either client apps, or backend apps, on a faster release schedule.

3) Package new features into services.

Assign services to teams

Some systems have hundreds or thousands of services running. They scale their organization by assigning each service to a team that is responsible for as much as possible about the design, development, testing, and operation of that service. It's really hard to design an organization to build and operate and support hundreds of different pieces of software. It's easy to assign those things to one team, and then add teams as needed.

Build teams around Tech Leads

Find a Tech Lead to take responsibility for a service. This eliminates project management layers.

You can build a team around a tech lead. You do not need a complete cross-functional team to begin with. The team can be any appropriate size, with the tech lead qualifying new contributors, making sure that code review and quality control is good, and answering questions. A practical team size is three people - the smallest size that accommodates vacations. You can rotate in new leads after they have some experience on the team.

Service leads will collaborate in real time with tech leads delivering end to end stories and features. Service leads should review and accept changes from the contributors that are delivering complete stories.

Tech leads release service changes as soon as they are ready. This process should be fast and responsive.

Two approaches to changing services

You will need to change your services over time, adding and removing interface components. However, you need to stay compatible with all of the clients that use the services. There are two approaches.

The "centralized" approach makes changes in all of the clients, at the same time that you change the service interface. To make this work, you will need a continuous integration system that tests the complete system with all clients, and finds any mismatches as early as possible. So, it is closely related to the centralized continuous delivery method.

The "distributed" approach uses services that are backwards compatible. You make new versions of the interface, but you keep the old versions, and you keep running the tests for the (recently expired) old versions. You will need this approach if you have components that are installed over time (e.g. browser and phone clients) or maintained by separated teams and partners and vendors with separated test systems.

Putting It Together

1) Fund complete programs or products. Keep your teams together and keep them improving.

2) Grow the program or product organically from a prototype. Analyze frequently. As it grows, shift strategies for team and task management, code management, test and release, and product management.

3) Divide the program or product into services, loosely defined as either software components or business services.

4) Find tech leads for each service, and for features with coherent stories. Build high performance teams around them with code review and strong quality control. They release changes as soon as changes are ready.

5) Unblock! contributors by reducing meetings, reducing batch processes, and providing a process for accepting code and changes from new contributors.

6) Provide all three paths to fixing the problem of dependencies - one person or team waiting for another. Do top-down planning for the things that you understand. Provide open peer to peer communication and escalation so that people identify and get the things they are waiting for. Encourage "fix it yourself" for important issues.

This will give you a development system that works at scale. Read the next chapter to find out how to use this powerful machine with effective planning and budgeting.

Continuous Enterprise

The Services Megatrend

We are in the middle of a change that is having a huge impact on software and on enterprise IT.

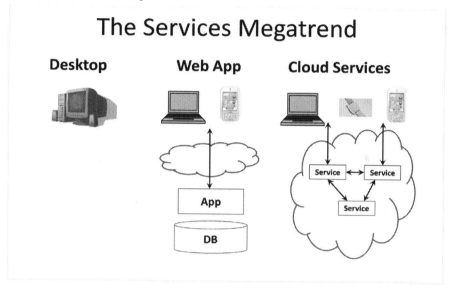

In the last generation of software, we built web applications that talk to desktop computers, and smartphones. These were often big applications with many features, running in one app server, with one database. We call this a "monolithic" design.

In the new generation, we are breaking those big apps into smaller apps that talk to each other using Web network protocols. We call them Web services. Users are increasingly picking small, best of breed applications and linking them together. Mobile phones and other devices talk directly to the service they need. Inside the Web apps that you see, front-end services are talking to back-end services. Applications may call other remote applications to get services they need. When you "login with Facebook" on a different app, or pick files out of Dropbox, you see these remote services in action. Monolithic apps are being broken into pieces that are easier to re-use, and easier to rapidly test and release.

The diagram above helps me understand some current buzzwords:

Consumerization of IT. Users are avoiding big enterprise apps and instead using smaller apps and services that each represent a best of breed experience in a narrow category.

Devices and Services. Big companies like Microsoft can link devices to their Web services in a single product package. Ultimately this becomes the "devices and services" architecture that will link most computing devices into one mesh.

The Internet of Things. Just add more devices, things like cars, thermostats, running shoes, etc., and you get the Internet of Things.

Big Data. All of those things stream out a LOT of data. That data gets stored in some services, analyzed in others.

Fast IT

Enterprise IT has split into two lanes. In the slow and steady lane, we have Core IT. Core IT is the traditional work of IT departments. It maintains systems that support the work of hundreds, thousands, or tens of thousands of people. They need systems that work reliably and have an assumption of security.

I got the "Core IT" term from Sacha Labourey of CloudBees, who was tactful enough not to call it "Slow IT." But Core IT is slow by design. It has strict requirements that slow it down. It is risk averse. It is usually funded with an annual budget, which is the way an organization tells its IT department to take at least a year to do anything.

In the other lane, we have Fast IT. Fast IT is the stuff that doesn't fit into an annual budget because it must be delivered fast and changed quickly.

Fast IT can take many forms, including:

- Mobile apps

- Marketing and sales sites and campaigns

- Everything that customers and partners are doing with your data and your API's

- All of the new products, software and systems that your own people are moving to public cloud infrastructure, where they can do new things with Continuous Agile.

Investment in Fast IT and SaaS is growing faster than the investment in Core IT. Through this process, many Core IT functions will eventually migrate into Fast IT systems on public clouds. This is the vision of "Web Scale IT."

Core IT is built with the engineering method. In the engineering method, we know our requirements. After we list out the requirements, we can engineer a system that meets most of the requirements. Then, we build the system.

Fast IT is built with the scientific method - experimentation. We don't know what will work, or we don't know how to make it work, so we do experiments to find out. We use Continuous Agile to keep this process moving, and we pay a lot of attention to measurable results.

I once read a study that compared engineers with scientists. It found that engineers often have extremely specialized knowledge about specific systems, and they can only talk about it inside their home organizations. Scientists work on more general problems, and they spend a lot of time communicating globally and sharing ideas. You will see this difference between the slow buildup of specialized expertise in Core IT, and the fast spread of techniques in fast IT with commercialization and consumerization.

On the shoulders of giants

Fast IT gets a lot of its value from Core IT. Core IT provides the unique data and product fulfillment that makes Fast IT interesting. Where does Fast IT get the prices for that hot online price comparison campaign? From Core IT. How does fast IT deliver the hot product? By asking Core IT.

An enlightened enterprise will put an API on its Core IT, and wrap it in Fast IT. From the point of view of Fast IT, Core API looks like a Web service.

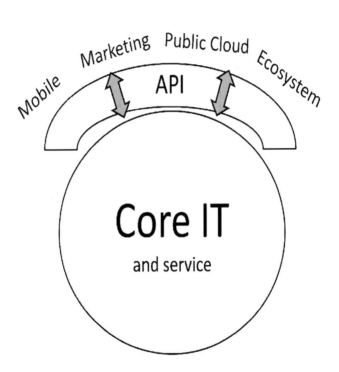

Matrix of Services

Matrix of Services, which I will call MAXOS, is the secret weapon that Silicon Valley is using to disrupt and destroy competitors.

I have seen the MAXOS structure in stories from Google, HubSpot, and Amazon. None of these companies uses traditional product management or textbook "Agile" methods. They have found something more powerful and more scalable.

To see the power of this method, we can compare a traditional online retailer with Amazon. The traditional retailer offers products and custom B2B ordering services through a monolithic application that is produced by a well-managed team of about 150 people. They use lean/agile techniques to produce a new release every six weeks. The operations team needs to be sure that their Web site, which brings in millions of dollars per day, doesn't have any reliability problems. Because it takes a long time to fully test a big app, they hold each release for three weeks of testing before they deploy it. So, the minimum time from idea to release is 9 weeks.

Amazon has more than 1000 service teams, each building and continuously releasing software. They release changes to a service, on average, once every 11.6 seconds. At any given time, 10,000 servers are being updated with new code. In the time that it takes retailer X to release one somewhat modified version of a monolithic application, Amazon has made more than 300,000 different improvements and adjustments.

I recently received a call from an Amazon Web Services competitor, who described his cycle time disadvantage as "an emergency."

How it works

Here is how MAXOS works. Software applications and infrastructure are divided into small services. For example, one service might render a Web page, and call a different service to get information about a product. HubSpot divided their online marketing service into 200 different services. Each service is built, tested, and operated by a small team. HubSpot has about 90 programmers, divided into 30 service teams. So, at HubSpot, each service team has three people, who take responsibility for 6 or 7 services.

Matrix of Services

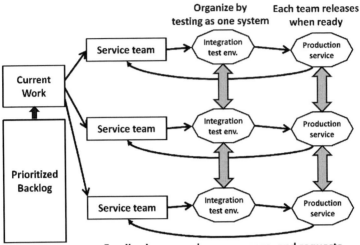

Each team takes complete responsibility for design, programming, testing, and release. They can release changes at any time. HubSpot reports that if you add up releases for all services, they typically release about 100 changes every day.

HubSpot teams also take responsibility for operations. HubSpot runs their matrix of services on 2000 Amazon servers, which they monitor for problems. If the monitoring system sees a problem with a particular service, it doesn't only notify an operations specialist, it also notifies every member of the service development team. That's a good thing, because with so many services, the operations specialist will not be able to understand and debug every one. This is a full implementation of the "DevOps" concept. HubSpot has a small number of operations specialists who build tools that the service teams can use to deploy, control, and monitor.

Each team receives a constant stream of feedback from their services about performance, errors, usage, and user-reported problems. If there is a problem, they see it and fix it.

Self-organizing

This structure has some remarkable self-organizing properties.

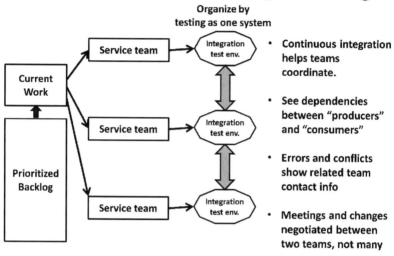

Coordinate Without Big Meetings

In a large project, it is often difficult to coordinate dependencies - the things that each team needs from other teams in order to fix something, or add a complete feature. Waterfall planners try to figure out all of the dependencies in advance on a big project chart - which never works. Scrum practitioners recommend a "Scrum of Scrums", a big meeting in which teams ask each other about their dependencies -which nobody wants to go to.

Service teams coordinate more happily through continuous integration. They release their changes into a shared test system. This system runs automated test scripts which uncover problems inside one service, or in the calls from dependent services. It can then notify the related service teams, and tell them who they need to talk to resolve the problems.

The continuous integration machine replaces a substantial amount of human planning and project management.

Teams are Largely Self-Managing

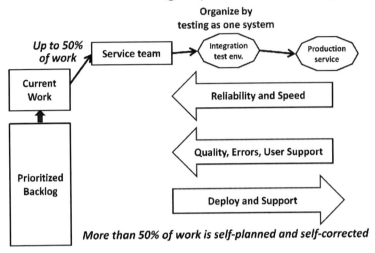

More than 50% of work is self-planned and self-corrected

A service team plans a large percentage of its own work, without any loop through a management or prioritization system.

Services teams know what they need to do because they are constantly receiving feedback from their services. They can plan their own immediate response to problems with reliability, speed, and quality. They do hands-on deployment and devops. They can plan medium-term responses to feedback from end users and their colleagues who are service consumers.

This system is more efficient than a system where each task has to go in a list for manager to look at and prioritize, since it does not consume management time. It also has a faster reaction time. Some scrum teams create an extreme version of planning lag by selecting a set of tasks in an iteration planning meeting, and then rejecting all new work for the next two weeks because it will disrupt their time estimates. Service teams can respond immediately to urgent requests.

Because service teams plan so much of their own work, they have a limited capacity to accept new requests. It is a harsh reality of software development that we spend much of our time making fixes, and it is unusual for any development team to have more than half of their time available for the development of truly new features and architectures. Self-managed teams turn this into an advantage. Service teams reduce work for managers and product owners, and free them up to focus on getting the most impact out of those new requests.

Scaling with Matrix of Services

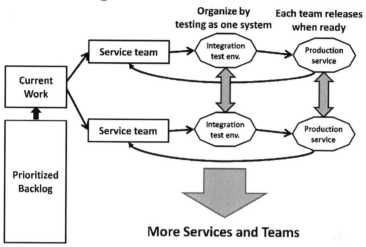

You can scale this organization by adding services, and adding service teams. Service teams have a simple structure built around a tech lead and programmers. There is a reduced need to plan and recruit for functions like QA, operations, and project management. MAXOS style organization can work for ten people, and work for 10,000.

Web-Scale IT

"Web-scale IT" is an idea from Cameron Haight of Gartner that describes how companies like Google, Facebook and Amazon use datacenters filled with massive numbers of cheap servers.

Three things come together to power these leading organizations:

- Web-scale datacenters with large numbers of cheap, replicated, virtualized servers

- Continuous Delivery

- A "Matrix of Services" organization

Web-scale is spreading as it becomes better, faster, and cheaper.

Already, Web-scale IT is being rented out. Anybody can go to Amazon Web Service and rent servers in their datacenter. Security-conscious enterprises can buy the capacity as a "hybrid cloud" protected by a virtual private network.

It's also being open-sourced. Initiatives like Cloud Foundry aim to deliver a complete set of open source software for a cloud datacenter. Docker has emerged as an exciting lightweight container for Web services. Facebook is sharing their datacenter designs and hardware designs as open source.

As a greater percentage of all business activity goes through online services, businesses that are organized around a matrix of services will dominate an increasingly diverse number of industries.

Powerful new hubs will emerge to support entire industries by providing a matrix of online services. These hub businesses may end up controlling big chunks of IT-intensive industries like finance and health care. Smaller companies will be very successful providing single, invisible Web services that get embedded into the larger matrix.

We can see how this works in 2013 by looking at Facebook. Facebook runs a huge Web-Scale IT operation with continuous delivery updating vast server arrays. They share services for login, comments, billing, payment, advertising, and plug-in applications - external Web services that use the Facebook API and user list. A whole industry with billions of dollars in revenue has grown up using these API's.

Government services are at the opposite end of the entrepreneurial spectrum. But, government efficiency will eventually be transformed by Web-scale IT. Government services are increasingly delivered through big software projects. These projects often suffer failures at the final integration stage, after huge amounts of money have been spent on development. As I write this, I am reading that the State of

Massachusetts canceled a contract to build a new tax return system, after spending $46M. Last week, the US Government turned on their health insurance exchange system after spending $400M - and it didn't work.

Continuous Agile and its related disciplines are designed to solve this specific problem by ensuring that no project reaches a late phase without being integrated and working well. While there are many obstacles to fitting Continuous Agile into a government procurement process, it will eventually happen, and the benefits will be huge. Governments that adopt Continuous Agile and a matrix of services IT organization will find that many of their online and offline services can be delivered more quickly and efficiently.

The road to an agile government may be long, but in the end benefits will come quickly and globally. Improvements will spread rapidly across the globe, because they can be so easily shared. A service that works in Massachusetts will work in most other states, and in some other countries.

MAXOS versus Scrum and SAFe

Scrum teams versus service teams

Scrum is currently the most popular way to organize agile development teams. Scrum teams are different from service teams in some important ways. A Scrum team has 5 to 10 people. It is multifunctional, meaning that it includes not only programmers, but experts in design, database, testing, and other functions that are required to deliver a complete feature or story. All of these team members should be co-located.

Building Scrum teams is a lot of work. It starts with the dreaded "culture change." It often requires coaching to explain roles and rituals. It requires moving people around to get a group of more than five in one place, every day. It requires the other parts of the organization to let go of their functional experts so that they can add the "multifunction" capabilities to the Scrum teams. After formation, scrum teams like to work together without team changes for a number of weeks to improve their estimating and get a consistent velocity.

If you have a high-performing Scrum team, you have a valuable asset. You can keep the team together, and use it as a large service team with expanded product management capabilities.

However, you will want to move the Scrum team to continuous response and continuous delivery. Scrum teams make "sprint" plans every two weeks, and then they stop accepting new work. So, their response time is at least two weeks. You want the fast response that you get from a continuous service team.

We frequently see service teams composed of three developers. This is the smallest team where someone can take a vacation. They are often all programmers - a tech lead, and two other developers that can learn to take over the tech lead role. Teams are small so they can be fast and efficient. They do not need to be multifunctional. They can be composed entirely of programmers. **In a continuous delivery process, programmers take a strong role**. Programmers call on design and test experts when they need them. The operations team provides tools for monitoring, test, and deployment, and programmers use the tools.

Building a service team is as simple as finding a tech lead, and adding collaborators as required.

Comparison

Size

- Scrum team size: 5-10
- Service team size: 2-8

Composition

- Scrum team composition: Multifunctional, with all roles required to deliver and release a complete "story"
- Service team composition: Programmers. They run the process and pull in other roles as needed. Operations provides tools.

Building the team

- Scrum team: Complicated to build. It often starts with coaches and "culture change." It includes a designated scrum master and product owner. People for all of the different functions (like design, QA, database) need to be pulled out of the functional parts of the organization. Then, the team runs some startup sprints to figure out their velocity and learn to estimate and release together.
- Service team: Build around a Tech lead. Release improvements on day 1.

Self-management

- Scrum team: Teams get product priorities every two weeks, and "self-manage" to plan and control their own two week iterations. Management needs to make sure that change requests go in a list and get prioritized in advance of the sprint planning meeting.
- Service team: Teams see extensive monitoring and feedback on their services. They handle fixes, improvements and requests without going through any management-level planning cycle. They accept new requests as soon as they have time.

SAFe and cadence-based management

SAFe, or Scaled Agile Framework, is a way of organizing Scrum teams to work on large projects. I will use SAFe as an example, because it matches a naive view of how to apply a traditional hierarchical organization to manage agile releases. Other enterprise management frameworks have a similar structure. You can learn more about SAFe from the wonderful diagram at ScaledAgileFramework.org.

SAFe uses the concepts of **hierarchy** and **cadence** to bring order out of chaos.

The hierarchy has three levels: portfolio, program, and project.

- At the portfolio level, senior managers decide what programs they want to fund, and what high priority goals they want to ask for. Senior managers in a MAXOS organization will do the same thing.

- Programs can match up with products or lines of business that have a unified deliverable. Programs can include from 5 to 100 projects (Scrum teams), and 50 to 1000 people.

- A project is the container for a Scrum team that can deliver complete features or stories.

SAFe and MAXOS have a similar hierarchy, except that SAFe uses Scrum teams on the bottom level, and MAXOS uses service teams.

SAFe relies heavily on cadence - a shared schedule that synchronizes everyone with a release, and a meeting. Cadence reminds me of the scene in the movie *Lord of the Rings*, where trolls beat on big drums to keep the orc army marching forward.

- Every ten weeks, all of the programs deliver an integrated system. Then, they have a big meeting where senior management presents the goals for the next iteration, and answers questions.

- Every two weeks, all of the teams in a program deliver a runnable product. Then they meet together, do their sprint planning, and have their "scrum of scrums" meeting where they make sure that other teams are building the things they need.

Naively, this meeting approach seems like a good idea. It guarantees that the organization will have a fully releasable system at least once every ten weeks. It guarantees that senior management gets a chance to communicate coherently at least once every ten weeks, and it motivates people by explaining the big goals. It guarantees that scrum teams will deliver runnable results every two weeks, and coordinate about the things they need from each other.

However, successful tech companies do NOT hold these big meetings. Why not?

- A system that relies on ten week planning and release cycles is too slow.

- Big meetings are difficult to organize, and expensive. Everyone has to come together in one location, or in a small number of locations with videoconferencing. Each meeting requires a day of work from everyone.

- The SAFe hierarchy and the Scrum teams have an intricate structure which takes time and management attention to build and organize. This costs time and money, and makes the organization less responsive.

Comparison

Top level planning

- SAFe: Executives plan at the Portfolio level to fund programs and product teams, not specific deliverables.

- MAXOS: Same

Top level communications

- SAFe: 10 week planning cycles with big meetings and global video connections

- MAXOS: Plan and communicate as needed

Integration cycle

- SAFe: 2 week integration cycles with big program-level meetings

- MAXOS: Continuous integration and release

Dependency management

- SAFe: Scrum of scrums meeting at least every two weeks, and more often if needed

- MAXOS: Continuous integration system continuously finds problems in dependent services and immediately notifies the related service teams to talk to each other.

Team structure

- SAFe: Scrum teams. Hard to build.

- MAXOS: Service teams. Easy to build.

Conclusion

Scrum and SAFe are logical first steps to plan agile releases in a traditional hierarchical organization. However, they are small steps, in a world where competitors make big leaps. Using Scrum and SAFe to compete with a MAXOS organization is not a winning strategy.

Realize Value Faster

If you work in a large enterprise, you have to balance competing requests from many business units, products, and product owners. You need to manage powerful personalities to achieve two goals.

1. Prevent your teams from being overloaded with too many projects at the same time. If they are overloaded, they can't take any new requests. If they have a bit of spare capacity, or have slots that open up frequently, they can respond to new requests and provide fast turnaround.

2. Motivate your product owners to divide their requests into small projects that deliver value quickly. You want them to learn to think incrementally.

In this chapter, **Damon Poole** explains how to achieve these goals. Damon understands how to use a lean philosophy to get more value out of large organizations. He introduced me to Kanban and continuous processes when he was the CTO and founder at code management pioneer AccuRev. He now works with Eliassen Group, consulting with enterprise customers and helping them become more Agile.

How to Realize Value Faster

Most enterprise software and IT groups are pressured into taking on too many projects at once. Even using Agile methods at the team level, they fall into the trap illustrated in the figure below. Here, two teams take on six projects and generate no value, and no revenue, for 18 months.

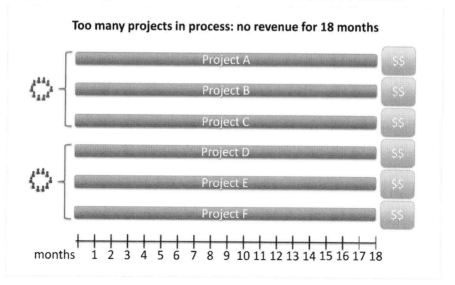

One solution is to limit the number of projects in process, ideally to the number of teams available. Each team focuses fully on one project, finishes it quickly, and starts generating revenue. Later, the teams move on to additional projects.

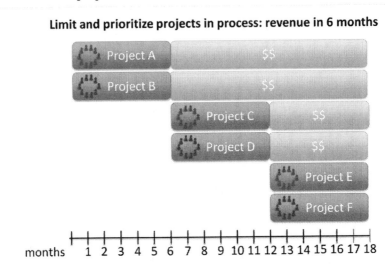

However, you may get huge arguments about which projects should go first. The business stakeholders for the second and third-ranked projects may object to being losers in a winner-take-all battle on priorities.

But there are ways to engage everyone in a constructive discussion – and to start generating value and revenue even sooner.

The first step is to work with the product owners to divide the projects into Minimum Viable Increments (MVIs). A Minimum Viable Increment is the smallest subset of a product which can be released, with a focus on the highest value. Viable in this case means that users will welcome its release rather than complain that there is not enough value.

Breaking projects into MVI's usually reveals that some sections of each project are bells and whistles that won't actually provide enough value to justify their implementation. When you are down to low-value functionality, it is better to drop those items from your plans and focus on other projects.

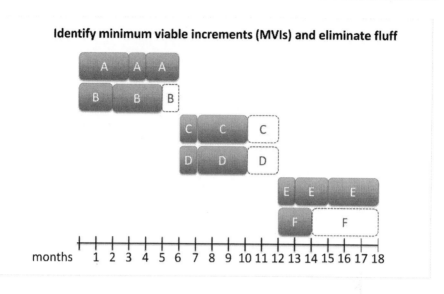

The next step is to set priorities among the MVIs. In the diagram below we see that although Project A and Project B, considered as a whole, are higher priority than Project C, there is a chunk of Project C that is a higher priority than some chunks of Project A and Project B.

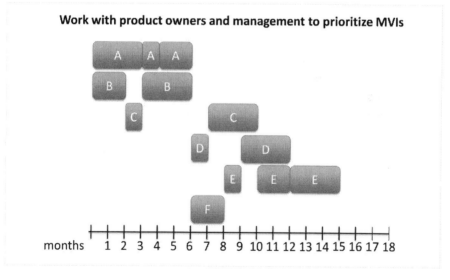

Now everyone is motivated to think in terms of MVIs. The smaller the MVIs, the more value the organization can provide and the more stakeholders can be satisfied over a given period of time.

You are now in a position to assign the prioritized MVIs to the available teams.

Assign MVIs to teams

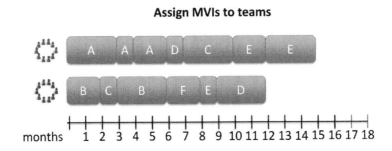

The resulting plan starts generating value as early as possible, maximizes revenue, and minimizes waste.

Result: generate revenue as early as possible

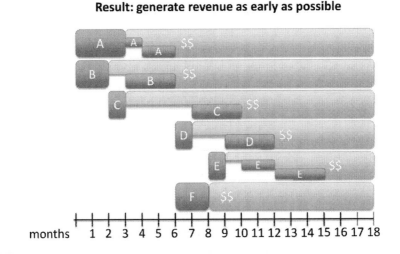

In this example everyone gets something. Projects A, B and C all start producing revenue after 3 months, and even Project E releases an MVI in 9 months.

This approach calls for flexible budgeting. It doesn't make sense to set project budgets annually if the mix and priorities of MVIs change frequently. You should work on shortening your budgeting cycles to semi-annually, quarterly, or even monthly. That gives you the chance to capitalize on the best opportunities for realizing value faster.

Future Vision

Innovation

The technology world is a cult of innovation. We see that innovation drives success in business, and in the larger economy. It is the building block of civilization.

Software is an almost-pure form of innovation. We call it "soft" because we can change it and reshape it easily. We are converting more and more of almost every product and service into software, because the softer something is, the faster we can improve it.

I can make one easy prediction: software will be a bigger and bigger piece of all of the goods and services that we produce. This has been a trend for 50 years, and it probably will continue for the next 50 years.

I will make some predictions about the ways that the next ten years will take us beyond Continuous Agile to increase speed, scale, and automation. Each step in the process is a straightforward challenge to engineers and organizers of our generation. Each step will provide a powerful competitive advantage for the businesses that can harness it.

The move to SaaS and MAXOS

Businesses will not be able to keep their old-style IT operations. If they keep the old ways, competitors will squeeze them out with faster innovation and aggressive, flexible pricing. We already see this happening in today's deflationary technology environment. All industries will eventually be affected. They can solve the problem by outsourcing their applications and data to SaaS providers. SaaS providers bring every customer up to a consistent level of innovation, scale, and cost management. SaaS providers run continuous delivery on Web-scale IT infrastructure, and they must compete globally on price.

For customized services, enterprises will run MAXOS — a service architecture with continuous delivery. Where MAXOS competes against old-style centralized planning, provisioning, and iterative development, it wins. Enterprise customers will integrate their SaaS providers into the MAXOS matrix as Web service providers. Some of them will build industry-dominating platforms of interconnected services. This will give startups new places to sell their services.

Clear division between Core IT and Fast IT

Enterprise IT users will draw a clear line between their old Core IT and the new Fast IT. They will systematically add API's to the Core IT, and bury it under new Fast IT running on mobile devices and commodity server farms.

The return of Core IT

If my product and service is increasingly based on software, I will want to own some software that gives me a competitive advantage. It will be increasingly clear where I need to invest in "Core IT" to run my business and build my products. I will be rewarded for big, multi-year investments in proprietary software and expertise.

The Empire of Code

Whenever you read this, people are coding. If they were to rise up in unison, they would form an empire on which the sun never sets. And who are the citizens of this empire? They are geeks. They think in similar ways. They may have been raised in a ranch house in Silicon Valley, a concrete apartment block in Kiev, a skyscraper in Shanghai, an igloo, or a mud hut, but when they sit down to work, they form one cultural unit. They live in physical countries where they study, carouse, date, raise families, and pay taxes just like their neighbors. However, they don't actually work in any particular location. They work "on the Web."

This poses some questions for governments. These geeks are a desirable demographic for governments because they are industrious people entering their best years for creativity, work, and paying taxes. Where should they pay taxes? Should they pay taxes where they work, or where their customers are, or where their employers are? If nations don't all have the same rules, there will be a gap. People will work in a country that taxes based on the location of the employer, and employers will locate in countries that tax based on where people work. It's not a coincidence that the companies that most successfully avoid taxes are global software companies like Google.

Geeks will seek out locations that respect their work environment. The world is currently not a friendly place for global teams that want to meet physically. To bring a multinational team together requires a lot of work to get visas for the meeting location. These visas typically state that visitors are not supposed to work without an additional work permit. There is currently no place in the world where a team can go and work together legally for more than a few weeks. I have started a "Software Sanctuary" project to solve this problem. We will make deals with host governments for a package of on-demand visas, work permits, and simple local taxation.

During the last 30 years, the old system of sovereign nations has spread out to include customs unions and currency unions and federations and autonomous regions and special economic zones. The empire of code is an interesting addition to this network.

Beyond Git and code

Code is king, and it has its servants. Git is a tool that makes it easy to move code around the Internet, and run the various code contribution and deployment workflows that we discuss in this book. It has become very popular and even essential since it was created seven years ago.

It will soon be replaced, although we don't yet know what will replace it.

Git uses a lot of manual commands to move and merge code between connected and disconnected users. However, most users are now connected. Outside of the coding world we use systems like Dropbox and gDrive that automatically detect and replicate changes between locations. We will also want automatic replication of code. We can imagine a system that grabs code changes as they are written. This system could test the changes on all possible merge paths, and continually tell us whether a change passes all tests and is releasable. This system could also see users that are working on the same piece of code, and notify them if they were making conflicting changes, in real time.

If we had a repository that could store and update complete running systems, we would not have to do quite so much work moving code around. "A Web service is the new executable," according to my friend Aaron O'Mullen. For a desktop or single server architecture, we compile an application into one executable file. In a service architecture, we do not compile one program and run it a a stand-alone executable. We build a whole "stack" or virtual machine, and run it as a Web service. When we do this, we send a lot of code and configurations back and forth from a code repository. If we want to build a new staging server, we first pull out the code that describes the server and run it. Then we pull out the code for our application and build the app. Then we pull out the latest configurations. This is why HubSpot has 500 Git repositories for 200 services. This machinery works, but it takes a lot of time to set up and maintain. Every one of those three processes (server build, application build, configuration) needs to be scripted and maintained by humans. The system will be a lot simpler and more efficient when we can version complete images or "containers." The repository will contain complete executable stacks in addition to code. Then, we can apply our review, merge, and promote workflows to make changes directly on the runnable systems, without the extra steps to build and configure.

Productivity comes from machines

We humans like to think we are getting smarter, but we are not. We are figuring a few things out, but we aren't getting smarter. So, how are we able to produce more code, faster, every year? We're using more machines, and bigger machinery. Farmers, coal miners, and automobile manufacturers increase their productivity dramatically as they employ bigger and better machines. Programmers get the same boost by using machines to search, build, test, scan, correct, and deploy their software. We can boost productivity by looking for places where we can use more machines, and do more different thing with machines.

Automated programming

There aren't enough programmers in the world to deliver all of the software we will need in the future. Only a small subset of the population enjoys programming and is good at it. Globalization has temporarily solved the problem by vastly increasing the number of educated, connected candidates. However, we will soon reach the limits of the new and expanded labor pool. We will solve the problem by replacing programmers with machines. Computers will program themselves.

I started working on automated programming and applying evolution to generate software in 1992. We didn't know in those days how to build big, useful systems, or how to merge the work of man and machine. Now the way is clear.

Machines can contribute code the same way that people contribute. In a continuous delivery process, each new bit of code gets written by a contributor, and then run through a process where it gets tested, reviewed, and accepted into the mainline version. Ten years ago, contributors were almost always people who worked on a professional team. Now, contributors often come from outside the company or from an amorphous open source community. With enough automated testing, and a simple review process, we can qualify their changes and feel confident accepting them. A machine can feed code changes into this same process. We will test and review their changes without knowing if they are people or machines.

The next step is automated bug fixing. I have recently spoken with several startup teams that are designing systems which fix bugs. Their machines will find automated tests that fail, and then find code changes that pass the tests. The computer uses a variety of approaches. They can look for bugs that fit a pattern, such as an incorrect variable name. They can search huge databases of similar code to find patterns that work. They can randomly make changes (mutations, in the language of evolution) until they get a good result.

In the bug fix process above, a human reviewer can accept or reject a change suggested by a computer. This is the building block of directed evolution, in which computers propose new versions, and humans pick the versions they like. Back in 1993, Karl Sims used directed evolution to create spectacular works of art. According to Sims, *"Genetic Images"* is a media installation in which visitors can interactively "evolve" abstract still images. A supercomputer generates and displays 16 images on an arc of screens. Visitors stand on sensors in front of the most aesthetically pleasing images to select which ones will survive and reproduce [through random mutation] to make the next generation." A reviewer from Wired wrote that "successive rounds...generate images of unbelievable beauty." Now this technique is used to design many types of products and packaging.

Directed evolution is used in online marketing, where computers make changes to Web pages or advertisements to find layouts that entice more users to click "buy." The autocorrect feature in a programmer's editor (like autocomplete in a search app) is another example of this approach. The editor shows an option for completing a line of code, and the programmer can accept the option, or keep typing. We can imagine a smarter version of this feature which pulls from a big database of prior code and templates, presents multiple options, and learns the programmer's style.

That brings us to less-directed evolutionary programming - an imitation of biological evolution. In evolutionary programming or genetic programming, computers make random changes to code and then run automated "fitness tests" to decide which versions to keep. Then they use a "genetic algorithm" to make new variations from the winners. This process continues until the code passes all fitness tests, or until computers go rogue and take over the world. The automated tests and test layers in a Continuous Delivery system can serve as a fitness test environment for genetic programming. However, there is one problem. Genetic algorithms tend to produce code that is unintelligible to humans. They don't think about code readability. They just generate garbage code and test it until they happen to find a piece of garbage that works better than your finely crafted code. So it's not a good idea to put evolved code into human-written software. We can safely incorporate this ugly-but-effective computer-generated code if we isolate it into a separate service. We can let the computers build and maintain complete services, which can run in our matrix of services beside services maintained by human teams.

I expect to see the computerized services start by taking on pattern recognition tasks. Pattern recognition tasks have the characteristic that it's easy to tell the computer what to do and specify the tests - "just find all of the pictures of cats" - but very hard for a human to write the code.The same tasks may be accomplished more effiiently by neural nets and neurorphic processes. Neural nets are another machine-learning technology that has been incubating since the 1980's and is now ready for packaging into services. We can even use evolutionary techniques to neural computers together with sequential computers.

Taken together, these techniques are the first steps a technology of innovation. By treating innovation as a reproducible technology that is based on evolution, we can incrementally improve it and increase its speed and scope.

Ray Kurzweil imagines a world where computers get faster and faster, and start learning faster and faster, until the process accelerates into an instant that goes beyond the human perception of time. He calls this the "singularity," driven by increased computing power. I doubt that you can achieve this effect just by increasing computing power. However, I believe that it is possible to solve a lot of problems by understanding and deploying the technology of innovation. We will start to understand the engine of creation, the evolutionary machinery that created life, that created computers, and that will create what comes next.

Authors

Andy Singleton

Andy Singleton is the founder of Assembla, where he leads an Agile software development team that crosses 15 countries. He has built more than 20 software and information products. He founded PowerSteering Software, a company providing project portfolio management software and Cambridge Interactive, an eBusiness developer. He has a BA in Applied Mathematics from Harvard.

Luca Milanesio

Luca Milanesio is the Director and cofounder of GerritForge, the leading Git and Gerrit competence center for the enterprise. Luca has over 20 years of experience in software development. He has facilitated the introduction of enterprise Code Review workflow in large enterprises worldwide, including major telecoms and banks. Luca is the author of Learning Gerrit Code Review and Git Patterns and Anti-Patterns.

Damon Poole

Damon Poole is a methodology and process improvement expert. He founded AccuRev, a leading provider of Software Development tools, and has consulted for Ford, Polycom, Xerox, Orbitz, Texas Instruments, Verizon Wireless and other industry leaders. Damon speaks at many major Agile and software industry conferences, writes frequently on Agile development, and is the author of Do It Yourself Agile.

Resources

Continuous Agile web site (consulting and professional services for development teams): www.continuousagile.com

Andy Singleton blog (thought leadership on continuous agile and innovation): www.andysingleton.com

Assembla web site (Agile planning, task management and collaboration tools for distributed teams): www.assembla.com

Comments? Suggestions? Ideas we should add to the book? Email Andy Singleton at andy@assembla.com

22049870R00132

Printed in Poland
by Amazon Fulfillment
Poland Sp. z o.o., Wrocław